My Big Fat Head

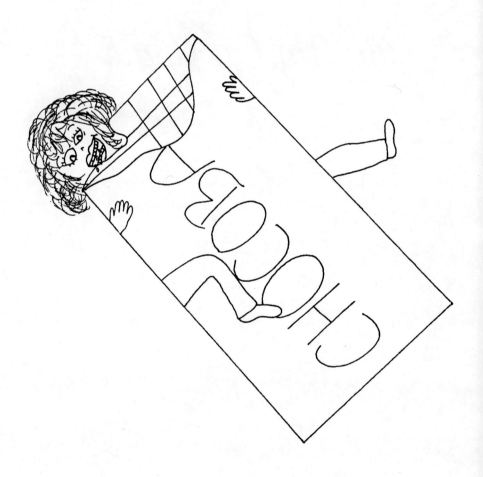

My Big Fat Head

Jodi M. Blase

Writers Club Press
San Jose New York Lincoln Shanghai

My Big Fat Head

Writers Club Press
an imprint of iUniverse.com, Inc.

For information address:
iUniverse.com, Inc.
5220 S 16th, Ste. 200
Lincoln, NE 68512
www.iuniverse.com

ISBN: 0-595-14795-X

Printed in the United States of America

*This book is dedicated to all those with heads
the size of watermelons.*

Epigraph

The mind is its own place, and it itself can make a heaven of hell, a hell of heaven.

—John Milton

Preface

I am a firm believer that what you keep inside your head festers in your body and spirit. Headaches, stomachaches, and heart disease are results of a soul kept prisoner from stress and fear. Stress and fear are primary candidates for addictions. Addictions such as bingeing and alcoholism are a result of the festering. I could no longer live a slave to addictions, obsessions, and weirdness without a fight. I wanted others to know that there was hope and life after addictions. Life is meant to be sloppy, messy and imperfect. We are meant to feel swerving gauges of emotions such as pain and despair, joy and elation—sometimes all in one day, sometimes all in one hour. Addictions mask the feelings and stagnate our souls. It is for the stagnated among us that I write.

Acknowledgements

I would like to thank Alcoholics Anonymous for allowing me to use the very important and all-powerful twelve steps in my book.

My gratitude to Anthony Rossetti from Of All Ages for his amazing foresight. Without his suggestion this book would not have been written.

To my editor, Lawrence H. Brown, thanks for everything!

My sisters Julie Havey and Kerry Bruno-Ruff, my brothers Thomas and David Bruno and my grandparents Anthony Bruno and Edna Cogan for their great support and good humor.

Thank you Denise Donahue, Agnes Mastropietro, Christine Landry, Karin Bourque, Denise Flannery, Laura Plummer, Amy Goober, Susan Wellnitz, and Jane Consolo for listening and reading and rereading and having the awful job of having to tell me where I needed to make changes to be understood.

To my three cherubs who knew mommy was writing a book and patiently played legos, drew next to the computer, or watched television even when it was ninety degrees-many thanks and much love.

To my husband who knew his wife was writing a book and gave me the space, time and support I needed.

Final thanks to my parents, Tony and Patricia Bruno, who have had the toughest job of all in having to read this book and see parts of my life they never shared with me. Parts that if known about at the time, they would've wanted to heal, but couldn't.

Introduction

I was told that for anyone to be interested in my big fat head I had to be a celebrity, a Ph.D., or a diet guru. I was told that I had to know someone to get anywhere with the information that I have to share. I was told to be credible I had to be a little more than a woman with her own experience, a little more than a housewife with three kids, a little more than your average Jo. In other words, more than I am. I thought about it for a while and decided that this was all a bunch of crap. I *am* the diet guru's client, I *am* the Ph.D.'s description on paper, and I *am* the celebrity without the big name. We are one in the same, only I'm not famous and thank God, no one has me under a microscope. I didn't date the President, I am not the Duchess of York, and I don't have my own drama series. I do, however, deserve to be heard. I know that my big fat head is just as credible as anyone else's, and those of you who own such a head know what I'm talking about.

My nature is black or white, no gray. I developed idiosyncracies throughout the years to help stabilize my big fat head. I checked and rechecked the door to make sure it was locked, turned the light switch on and off four times, washed my hands four times, did just about everything in fours. So I'm weird. I'm not ashamed of who I am anymore. I'm not original, that's for sure. Everyone has some bit of weirdness in them. You'd be hard pressed to convince me otherwise. I have yet to meet someone, anyone, who doesn't have an addiction or a quirk or a bit of obsessiveness ingrained within them. Me? I have to either tell it like it is by emotionally purging myself or suffer internally for keeping silent. An issue, quite clearly derived from my big fat head. I have to be painfully clear about my views, even if they offend. For the offending of others will be minimal to the survival of my sanity.

Definition

FATHEAD (fat-head) adj. An intolerable loneliness, an emptiness as deep as an eternal landfill, a constant committee of indecision swimming in one's head. Its main purpose is to incapacitate with an overabundance of negative thought processes. Its goal is self-destruction of true human instincts. Outlets include food addiction, alcoholism, gambling, obsessively cleaning or shopping or any other act done ad nauseum. Not a part of the brain, but a seepage that occurs at a young age (if not birth) and continues until it has been discovered and disabled.

Out Of Recovery

What Is Fat, As In Fat Head And Fat Body?

If fat were viewed under a microscope, I don't think scientists would find just adipose or fatty tissues of the body, or whatever it is they see. Under closer observation I think they'd find hidden layers, like the rings of a tree that would tell how old it is, the life it has experienced and the trauma sustained. Inside each layer wrapped between the fat unable to escape its lardy goop they would see tears, joy, sadness, excitement, loneliness, boredom, fear and denial. And if, with a paring knife, the fat were whittled away, layer by layer, they would find the pathology from which the vicious cycle all began.

I often wished I could have unhooked the side of my waist and peeled off the fat. Or scraped the fat off my stomach with one of those ice scrapers you use to clean snow off your car. I look at obese people and wish I could unlatch something on their body that would instantly peel off their fat, thus peeling off their pain. The hanging jowls or stomachs look surreal to me, like a costume. And in a way, it is a costume, hiding the real person inside. It used to astound me to hear, "love yourself for who you are." How could I love my legs rubbing together, or the chaffing during shorts season, or the sweating or the extra large clothing? How could I love myself but weigh so much? Isn't loving oneself taking care of oneself? That doesn't include kidney disease, gall bladder problems, or early heart disease, does it? Not that it's wrong to be happy and fat. It's absolutely fine, for someone else. I commend people who are two hundred pounds and full of self-esteem. People who write books declaring that being heavy isn't the end of the world. I do believe this is true myself. Being heavy or being thin doesn't make the person you are. I have been both and believe me, the only change you receive is physical, which has its rewards, but doesn't fix anything inside the lardy goop. Mentally and spiritually you have to be fit to be happy in whatever your size. But for me being overweight was like slow death. And the death wasn't from the fat itself, but from the feelings the fat caused. Or should I say, the foods I ate that caused the feelings that caused the fat. Self-love was a foreign expression, similar to a chant one hears on the Discovery channel from a tribal community in the jungle. It didn't make any sense to me. It was at this point my brain informed me how I had been living all these years. It told me I had to change the way I ate to change the way I felt. The food was my hiding place, as is alcohol or drugs for other people.

You Are Here

You think you're you until one day it's like you're standing in front of the directory at the mall staring down at the arrow marked YOU ARE HERE. You want to find the shoe store and all you can see is a huge color-coded directory with arrows and numbers pointing in every direction. You look at the map. The shoe store is 2101 green. That means it's on the second floor. The diagram is shaped funky, like a U wrapped around another U and the colors are entwined and the numbers are so close together you can barely discern them. Great. Unless you've memorized the stores that are around the shoe store you end up looking up and down the mall for landmarks wondering about the useless directory. That's what my life was like. I began to wonder where I was and where I was going. Everything was the same: my job, my kids, and my husband. I loved my kids, liked my job and adored my husband, but something was missing. So I started to trace back through the events that led me to where I was at that moment. Back through car pools and first words and diapers and job changes. Back through relationship changes before children and marriage, back to when I was alone with nothing to do or no one to worry about; back when the world was indeed my oyster. Suddenly I realized what was missing-ME. I had one problem stopping me from truly being happy. I had an addiction, (my favorite addiction of many) and it was out of control.

I don't think of my addiction as having any less importance than that of heroin addiction or alcoholism. The funny thing is when a heroin user kicks the habit, we would never think of saying, "it's o.k. once in a while", "live a little", "go ahead and cheat", "it's the holidays." But when one informs people that they are dieting or changing their eating behaviors all you hear is, "it's o.k. once in while", "live a little", "go ahead and cheat, "it's the holidays". You think there's a big difference between heroin and food? I don't. They both cause a high and a feeling of wanting more when the high is over. They both are craved in such a way that you'll do anything to get your hands on more. And when "more" is gone, it's still not enough.

I treated food like a drug and couldn't stop eating even when I wanted to. Not even when my stomach was crying for me to stop. Not when the fat on my waist was hanging over the tops of my jeans. Not when I could taste sour food in my mouth because I had eaten so much I was regurgitating. Not when my big fat head was oozing out my ears. And especially not when I truly loathed the weak, pathetic person who was staring back at me in the mirror.

This is the story of my life. But it could be your life, or perhaps the life of someone close to you. Nothing extraordinary has happened to me that hasn't already happened to someone else. No demons from my past could explain how I came to be the person I am today. That's not important anyway. What is important is what I decided to do about it and how I ended the pain inside my body, head, and soul.

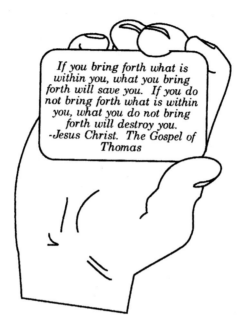

> *If you bring forth what is within you, what you bring forth will save you. If you do not bring forth what is within you, what you do not bring forth will destroy you.*
> -Jesus Christ. The Gospel of Thomas

What I've Tried

I've tried everything to lose my weight. I've done the diet program shuffle, herbal protein drinks, three day diets, and whatever the diet fad of the moment was. I purchased every magazine that said, "Lose 10 pounds in a week" on the cover. I've binged, starved, tried to vomit, and took laxatives. I went to gyms and worked out, lifted weights, took long walks in the wee morning hours and longer walks in the evening. I've consulted doctors and nutritionists and have been given medical diets to follow.

I tried to be happy being overweight. I couldn't do it. Being overweight ruined my life. Eating sugar changed my mood and how I felt about myself. Mentally and chemically, I couldn't be happy.

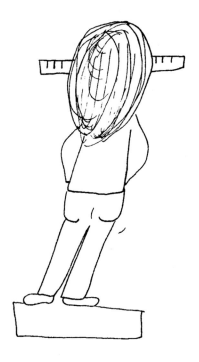

What's A Food Scale?

I started my first official diet at sixteen years old. The meeting was held in a synagogue across from a ballpark. I had heart failure the first time we pulled up to the synagogue. There were three or four baseball games going on and the park was filled with kids my age. I ran from the car to the door as quickly as possible, keeping my face forward to avoid being seen.

Everyone in the diet program was at least thirty years old. I was weighed and then given a booklet with my name, date, and weight written on it. Every week I would have to wait in line to get weighed. My weight would then be recorded in this booklet. I wasn't too keen about stepping on a scale with other people around. The scale was positioned so that the people behind you weren't able to read your weight. I noticed, however, that if the line swayed a little to the left you could see the weight perfectly. So when it was my turn I tried to lean in the general direction of the line to try and block the view of the numbers on the scale.

My goal weight (the weight I wanted to attain) was recorded across from my top weight (the weight I originally was). I attended a few meetings before telling my mother that everyone was too old. I said I would continue with the diet regimen on my own. I weighed my portions as I had learned at the diet program (a four ounce piece of meat was as big as the size of the palm of your hand), and tried to eat a contained diet. I began eating a sit down breakfast instead of a doughnut on the way to school. I'd skip the school lunch and eat when I got home at 2:30 p.m. A typical lunch consisted of a tuna melt on English muffins with tomato and cheese followed by a piece of fruit. I managed to lose ten pounds in a month following this plan. Then I strayed, first by eating diet desserts, then by ignoring my portions. The portions became larger and larger and never seemed to satisfy my hunger. I switched to eating regular desserts instead of the diet desserts, or doubled the portions of the diet desserts. A month after I had lost the ten pounds, the weight was back on. And for the life of me, I couldn't figure out why. I never saw my old behavior coming. It sort of sneaked in sideways when I wasn't paying attention, and before I knew it, I was fat again.

Life With A Blankie

As human beings we develop comfort objects. When we are young it's a blankie, a pacifier, a thumb or perhaps a stuffed animal. When we mature we get hooked on cigarettes, drugs, alcohol, food, exercise or any compulsive behaviors, such as perfectionism. A consistent reinforcement of our comfort object keeps us in check and stabilizes our being. But take it away and we become angry, irritated, anxious individuals who "need our fix", and will do most anything to get it. Have you ever seen a child who has lost his blankie? I have, and it's not a pretty sight. The child goes berserk upon realizing that his blankie is missing. First, a look of panic passes over his face as his eyes jut around the room like radar. This is quickly followed by incessant babbling of "where blankie, where blankieeee." Then a fit of rage as the cries grow louder "BLANKIEEEEE!!!!" followed at last by tears of helplessness. I babysat a child who had a blankie. When I thought he was sound asleep I washed the filthy thing so it would be clean when he woke up. Unfortunately he woke before the blankie was dry and I found him screaming for the blankie smashing his head back and forth against the portable crib. I quickly got the blankie out of the dryer and handed it to the child whereupon his whole world changed. He became subdued and happy. All over a piece of cloth. You see, he needed that blankie to soothe his mental state of health. That piece of cloth meant something to him, something far deeper than I could have possibly imagined. That's how I felt when I didn't get the foods I craved or desired: helpless. I allowed my desires for food to direct my thoughts and rule my actions.

Addicted To Food

My big fat head had filled up fairly fast, four years old being a safe estimate. Food provided me with a false sense of security. Food was my blankie.

I was four years old when eating became almost too enjoyable. I say four years old because I can't quite remember what I was like at three years old, but at four, it is pretty clear, at least in the basics. I loved food. I loved the way it looked and smelled. I loved the way some food was crunchy and some food was mushy. I loved that some food was hot and some cold. I loved that chocolate melted in my mouth and ice cream froze my lips. Eating was like a shot of Valium. Sugar was my salvation. The thought of sweet sugar filling up my mouth and activating my salivary glands in a way nothing else could was almost orgasmic. Sucking on a fudgiscle as the wet pop melted around my mouth was simply satisfying. Feeling sweet foods slipping down my throat as all of my senses worked overtime to make it linger. As it helplessly faded away into my stomach, I felt a sheer tease…until the next bite. My life was comprised of crunch, chew, and AHHHH! The image that comes to mind is that of a junkie shooting up. Only I'm the junkie, and I'm mainlining sugar.

From a very early age, I have thought of food as one would think of another person. I gave food the power of life. I used it as a sedative, a lover, a mother, a father, and a confidant. I ate to hide the things I felt, the secrets I kept and the lies I told. I

chose to hide behind the food and become invisible, never letting the real me shine through. I just couldn't stop eating no matter how much I wanted to, no matter how much pain it was causing me. This is the story of how my very best friend became my worst nightmare.

Where It Took Me

Overeating has deprived me of many of life's gifts, or should I say, I have allowed overeating to deprive me of many of life's gifts. So what's a little fat, eh? What's ten, even fifteen pounds of extra weight? It's not like half the population of America could use to drop a few pounds, right? Don't you feel better when you're stressed out and you eat that sundae or that bag of chips? Why do you suppose that's so? I ate that sundae and felt like someone had deflated the air out of a very full tire.

When I was seventeen years old I was working at a doughnut shop. One of the regulars came in and was telling me it's hard to quit smoking because of, among other things, cilia. Cilia are little hair-like processes that extend from a cell surface. They are found in your nose, throat and lung cavities and what they do is help move foreign particles or mucous along so that nothing festers in those areas. Smoking causes the cilia to lose elasticity and flatten out which prevents phlegm from moving along, leaving room for infection. He went on to say that when you quit smoking the cilia begin to rejuvenate and itch, but not an itch you are conscious of. This itch registers as a craving in the brain, which is why it is so difficult to stop smoking. As he was telling me this he was lighting a cigarette. That's how I feel my binges on food happen. When I eat certain foods something chemical occurs in my brain that I register as a craving. Once I start eating, I can't seem to stop because I'm filling this craving that began as an emotional binge but turned into a chemical binge. Chemically speaking, eating a sundae was just as effective as taking a good stiff drink.

I can say that many situations may have aided in my fear and in my lack of confidence, but I can't blame any particular thing or person. For example, some people can experience a life of torture and hell and still come out healthy, functional human beings. Other people can experience a relatively smooth life and for some reason carry in them a feeling that somewhere, something is not quite right. They wait and wait all of their lives for that not quite right thing to happen, often missing most of life's gifts. My husband lives by the theory that if you die, you die. I asked why it didn't concern him or make him afraid to think of death and he replied, "Because I'll be dead, so it really won't matter, now will it. Everything that I've left behind will take care of itself." O.k., maybe that's logical. But me, I'm more The Murphy's Law poster child.

My addictions developed because I felt a lack of control over my life situations. I couldn't accept life for what it was, a learning experience and a process. I got uneasy over the process part because it entailed feelings and working through things. Working through things wasn't so much the scary part as was having to feel what you were working through. I've since learned two things about feelings: 1. Feelings aren't facts. Just because we feel something doesn't make what we are feeling a true reality. 2. You don't have to do anything with your feelings except to let yourself feel them.

My favorite addictions brought counterparts with them: fear, doubt, and low self-esteem. Food filled the emptiness that these beasts brought upon me. Without food I surely would have perished many years ago.

But with it, I have been a prisoner in my own body, trapped under rolls of fat, the real me lurking somewhere in the darkness.

What It Felt Like

I have been anywhere from ten to forty pounds overweight during the course of my life. The older I got, the more weight would creep on. What was once pudge soon turned into fat. The most prominently painful years are those of adolescence. Today I look at overweight teens and get a sinking feeling right in the pit of my stomach. The feeling makes me nauseous and leaves me wanting to cry. I know what these overweight teens are up against. I know the physical and mental damage they will sustain by being overweight.

My mind is filled with whirling thoughts of my youth as I try to restrain myself from approaching an overweight teen and telling them, "I know the boyfriends I lost and the parties I missed. I remember knowing the answer, yet being unable to raise my hand in a classroom full of kids. I remember getting my first pair of "Bonjour" corduroy jeans for Christmas when I was thirteen years old and discovering they were much too tight. The fact that bellbottoms, halter-tops, and hip huggers didn't look right on a chubby teen didn't make matters any better. Sitting with my thighs tight so no one would see the worn out patch marks on my corduroys, I remember the excess of makeup and hair primping as if looking perfect from the face up would somehow compensate for the neck down. Loose, baggy clothes were all I felt comfortable in. Physical ailments were plenty: back pain, stomachaches, and bronchitis; all from overindulgence and self-abuse. I can remember the comments, ("too bad she's such a big girl, she's so pretty", and " you sweat a lot because you're heavy"). I remember the colleges I didn't apply to and the extracurricular activities I declined to partake in, all due to my weight. I've felt the pain of faking my menstrual period every week to get out of swim class and not receiving any carnations on Valentine's Day. Going to the doctor's and having to deal with the 'look' from the nurses when you were weighed in, when you're practically naked on the scale and still 165 pounds. The incredible, gnawing fear of never being able to be 'normal' that remains with you day after day. The feeling that life is not enjoyable, but survivable." I want to tell them that the food will swallow them up until they are empty. But I can't say any of this because I can't bring myself to look at the face that will be receiving these words. For it is my own. No one could've prevented me from eating as much as I wanted. So I forget what I want to say to this overweight kid because I am back in my own head and fifteen years old walking in a slouched position covered by long tee shirts and flannels, my poodle-permed hair in front of my face that is looking at the ground. I am walking into my house and heading straight for the refrigerator. I am preparing to eat whatever is available just to ward off any raw feelings that may have been elicited from a day in the life of an adolescence plagued by emotion. And the funny part was that I wasn't even *aware* of the damage I was doing on a rational level. I thought that eventually what I felt, who I was, would somehow take care of itself. I never considered, not for a moment, the impact my fat head would have on me over time.

The majority of my life previous to and after adolescence was filled with more eating, hiding, wanting to change, but unable to. So, how did it feel to go through life overweight and with a big fat head? Insatiable.

Never Enough

Saying there was never enough food for me is a given, but there also was never enough of anything else. If I just got a brand new typewriter, my friend had a better one. If my mom bought me a brand new coat for Christmas, my friend got a better one. If my sister and I got the same toys in different colors, her color was better. Nothing filled me up. I compared who I was, what I owned and how much I knew with who other people were, what they owned and how much they knew. If a friend of mine had a better Barbie than myself it would mean her WHOLE life was better than mine. To be grateful for what I had, I wasn't. I was the most slighted person on the face of this earth! Food came closest to filling the void. I would stuff myself full and still want more. When bigger cookies came out, I wanted the bigger cookies. I wanted the largest sundaes, the biggest apples, the most cereal, and the foot long hot dog. At a carnival I'd watch as the woman made cotton candy. I always felt she gave me the smallest one of the bunch. I wanted to scream I want it BIGGER, give me MORE! But as I said, it wasn't just in food that nothing was ever enough; it was in everything. Not the easiest way to choose to live one's life.

But You Could Die From It

A couple of years ago I was exercising at an all women's gym. On my way out I began reading the bulletin board. There was a request for volunteers to help people who were being treated by the Massachusetts Eating Disorders Association. Knowing that I could be of help because of my own personal background, I decided to call the number. A young student answered the phone and began asking me a series of questions: was I overweight now, what is my experience, why do I want to help. I told her that I needed to lose around 15 pounds, that I had background experience in nutrition and had worked with people with mental illness in the past who were also battling weight problems. I then told her about my own past and why I believed others would benefit from my experience. What follows is the rest of our conversation to the best of my recollection:

Girl: The population I have consists of overeaters, anorexics, and bulimics. Is there a specific group you'd prefer to work with?

Me: Probably overeaters.

Girl: Would you be uncomfortable if you were placed with an anorexic?

Me: No, but I'm not sure that I have anything to offer. We (myself and an anorexic) seem to be at different ends of the spectrum. But I wouldn't mind trying. (At this point in my life I actually envied anorexia and believed that the whole anorexia thing was not as serious as compulsive overeating.)

Girl: I will call you and let you know as soon as I come up with anything.

A few days later she called me again:

Girl: I have someone for you who is overweight, but she also has a mental illness.

Me: You have no one else in your program that doesn't have a mental illness?

Girl: I have anorexic and bulimic individuals, but I thought about it and considered the fact that since you are an overeater and not one of them, they may consider you a threat. They might think that you are trying to get them fat.

Me: Oh, I see. It's too bad there aren't many overeaters in the program.

Girl: Well, we deal mostly with anorexics and bulimics because they have a life threatening illness. Overeating is not as serious as this.

I became annoyed with the fact that a college student working for the Massachusetts Eating Disorders Association thought only anorexics and bulimics had a life threatening disease. Obviously being an overeater was not as serious as starving yourself or purging your food. But it was to me and I said:

Me: But it *is* a life threatening illness. If you are obese you can develop kidney disease, liver problems, heart disease. It may not be as fast as dying from anorexia, but it could kill you eventually. I think that people tend to overlook...

Girl: (abruptly) I'll call you if there is anyone else.

I never heard from her again. She sounded defensive and at a loss for words. I was merely trying to point out that no matter how you treat food, it's all dangerous in the end; it will affect you not only mentally, but also physically and spiritually. This eventually led to me wonder whether or not overeating was considered an illness as is anorexia and bulimia. I called a few girlfriends who were social workers and asked them to look in their DSM books (diagnostic medical terminology, features, and criteria) to see if overeating criteria were defined in any way. In DSM-III overeating is not stated, but anorexia and bulimia are. In DSM-IV there was something. It wasn't with anorexia or bulimia diagnoses, but at the back of the book in an appendix titled, "Criteria Sets and Axes Provided for Further Study." They titled it "Binge-eating disorder." Here are the research criteria for binge-eating disorder:

A.   Recurrent episodes of binge eating. An episode of binge eating is characterized by both of the following:

(1) eating, in a discrete period of time (e.g., within any 2-hour period), an amount of food that is definitely larger than most people would eat in a similar period of time under similar circumstances

(2) a sense of lack of control over eating during the episode (e.g., a feeling that one cannot stop eating or control what or how much one is eating)

B. The binge-eating episodes are associated with three (or more) of the following:
    (1) eating much more rapidly than normal
    (2) eating until feeling uncomfortably full
    (3) eating large amounts of food when not feeling physically hungry
    (4) eating alone because of being embarrassed by how much one is eating
    5) feeling disgusted with oneself, depressed, or very guilty after overeating
C. Marked distress regarding binge eating is present.
D. The binge eating occurs, on average, at least 2 days a week for 6 months.
    Note: The method of determining frequency differs from that used for Bulimia Nervosa; future research should address whether the preferred method of Setting a frequency threshold is counting the number of days on which binges occur or counting the number of episodes of binge eating.
E. The binge eating is not associated with the regular use of inappropriate compensatory behaviors (e.g., purging, fasting, excessive exercise) and does not occur exclusively during the course of Anorexia Nervosa or Bulimia Nervosa.

How the criteria work is that you need to have both 1 and 2 of A category, three or more of B category, C D, and E. If you meet the criteria, you are most likely a binge-eater. Although this was found in the Appendix (B) for further study, I'm content that it is being researched at all. I have always been confused by the paradox that although I have made the choice to eat certain foods, I have felt out of control when eating them. It's like that potato chip commercial; "Betcha can't eat just one."

Even Fat People Are Prejudiced Against Fat People

Depending on how fat you actually are, you can be prejudiced against someone who is fatter. You may be heavy, but shit, you aren't near as fat as 'so and so'. I am one of the biggest offenders. I used to secretly mock obese people. I wanted to ask them what was the matter that they couldn't stop eating. I wanted to say, "doesn't it bother you to be this fat, have you no control?" In reality, the disgust that I saw in them was the disgust I felt in myself. I have come to realize that the people that I become most belligerent toward are the people that remind me of myself.

Although I never became that heavy physically didn't mean I didn't feel that heavy mentally. Being anywhere from 10-40 pounds overweight has consumed my life. I could be 10 pounds overweight and feel 200 pounds overweight in my head, my head weighing 100 pounds on its own standing.

Society has dictated that being fat or even a few pounds overweight is not a good thing. I believe it's one of the greatest prejudices that we as human beings will have to confront.

The Beginning Of The End

The year was 1995. I was twenty-eight years old living in an apartment below my grandfather. This would be the first time I would cook any sort of food for a holiday get together. In the spirit of the holiday I decided to serve sugar cookies shaped like Easter eggs, at least two dozen. Even though it was only dessert and not the main meal, I was eager to be perfect. Perfectionism, another of my addictions, though not my favorite, is a royal pain in the ass. It is horrible to feel that the fate of all mankind rests on your shoulders, and on the decision of what you are going to serve for dessert.

I have never liked or enjoyed the holidays. I liked the idea of what the holidays were supposed to represent: families smiling together drinking Maxwell House coffee, eating chocolate cake, reminiscing over remember when's, putting their troubles aside for the sake of what the actual holiday itself symbolized. But my idea of holidays and the actual event were two separate entities. Holidays made me anxious, over-excited and over-stimulated because they never, ever met my big fat head's expectations. Immediately after grace was said, I filled my plate and ate with a vengeance. When I was ready to implode, I stopped eating so that I could breath in and out without too much discomfort. At dessert time the whole routine would begin again. I hung around the dessert table like a vulture picking at each dessert until I felt sugar sick. That's what the holidays meant to me, one uncontrolled day of bingeing beyond a stomachache, beyond indigestion, beyond belief.

For two days previous to Easter I practiced making sugar cookies. Because of continual 'taste tests' I had to make twice the allotted frosting. It was mechanical, a scoop for the cookie and a scoop for me.

Everyone said the cookies were delicious. I myself couldn't look at the cookies after two solid days of bingeing on the frosting. My sister's bunny cake, however, was a different story. After taking sliver after sliver, I grew tired of going back and forth from the kitchen to the living room. I finally gave up and sat in front of the damn cake and ate until I was full. The rest of the day was spent eating sugar, periodically combating the nausea I felt from the sugar overdose with food. I don't recall any conversations I had with any of my relatives or when they came and left. I just remember the desserts and wished everyone would disappear so I could eat in peace and quiet. After all, this was personal; my relationship with sugar was synonymous to a relationship with a person. It was committed, loyal, and full of lust. I was in love with sugar—it controlled my day, my mood, and my sanity. In a nutshell, it had me by the throat.

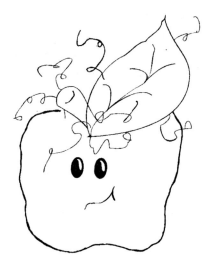

Something's Got To Give

I exercised faithfully into the summer. I varied from 154-157 pounds. I could live with 154 pounds, but for some reason, 157 pounds was unacceptable. Funny how three measly pounds can become so upsetting. I knew there were thin mothers out there, I just assumed that they starved themselves or were naturally thin. How else could they maintain their weight?

I joined the local all women's gym and began exercising three times a week for one and a half-hour sessions. The other two days I would walk an hour with the kids, pushing the carriage up and down hills. It appeared that all my hard work was in vain because I seemed to be exercising just to maintain my 154-157 pounds. It was an enigma to me. It never occurred to me to cut back on my intake of foods. I ate fat free foods, and all I could. I considered fig cookies, graham crackers and pretzels "free" foods. I snacked on them all day thinking it was harmless.

I mean, how much weight could they put on me? My big fat head told me, "No weight at all, go ahead, enjoy!"

At the gym I would watch the thin women work out in their little spandex body suits. I wore baggy sweats and a long tee shirt. After exercising I would reward myself with a half cup of fat free frozen yogurt. Now and then I would add fat free chocolate syrup to the ice cream, but not too much; calories, you know. In the beginning I measured an actual half-cup of frozen yogurt, but after a while I just opened the half gallon, poured in the chocolate syrup and ate straight from the container. Sometimes I'd eat a teaspoon full of syrup straight up for a quick rush. The frustration I felt each time that I stepped onto the scale was one of self-hatred and loathing for my weaknesses.

My son's first birthday was in July of 1995. I found myself stressing out over the smallest details; mainly focusing around the food I was going to serve. Turns out there was plenty of food and dessert to go around, although I was a bit nervous about the cake. It was a *Winnie-the-Pooh* cake that seemed too small to feed everyone. Luckily, none of the adults wanted any and there was even a small amount left over until later in the day when I got my hands on it. While I was eating the cake I recall thinking, "this cake isn't too good." But you know what? I still ate it.

I remember my son's first birthday not just as his big day, but mine as well. It was pivotal in helping me decide once and for all I had to stop abusing my body the way I had been doing for 24 years. From Christmas of that past year up until my son's birthday in July I had been uncontrollably bingeing on sugar products at least twice a week. In previous years, I would binge from one week prior to one week after the holiday for a total of three weeks of on and off bingeing. Then the bingeing would be over and I would begin my latest diet and exercise regimen. Now it seemed Christmas to July was one big holiday feast with only sporadic breaks. These binges were hard enough to overcome emotionally during the holiday season, never mind a good six months of bingeing. And with the bingeing came my other behaviors: doing everything in fours, fantasizing, over obsessing, and pain-in-the-ass perfectionism.

It would start the same way every day. I would get up thinking that this was going to be the day I would control myself and eat normal, balanced meals. There would be no sugar today. By 10:00 a.m. I would have a couple of fig cookies or graham crackers. Soon, I was eating a package of graham crackers, or a strip of fig cookies. Before I knew it, it was lunchtime and I was still eating! So, figuring I've blown it for yet another day, I decided to start my diet tomorrow.

After dinner, I would wait for the 8:00 o'clock sitcoms and make myself a nice bowl of ice cream with syrup or fat free cool whip (calories, ya know) and sit stupefied in front of the television. Engrossed in the faux lives of the characters, I wished I could just jump into the television and be a part of it all.

Any human who dared to bother me in the midst of my eating was destined for doom. I did not take being disturbed too lightly. As I have said before it isn't easy being me. It took a lot of effort to concoct my food and plan my dates with myself on the sofa in solitude. The harsh world was far, far away. I didn't want any conversations; I wanted to be alone with my sugar. I began to realize that this was my life everyday, all day. How was I functioning for my kids and my husband?

It wasn't until July that my brain pushed its way through the lardy goop and informed me it was over. My big fat head had seen its day. I knew it was time because food didn't even have a taste anymore. Cookies might as well have been cardboard for all I knew. I couldn't find anything that would quell this hunger. It was as if I had gone over the top of enjoyment and fallen in my own personal hell with food, especially sweets. I was ready to call Switzerland for their chocolate since ours wasn't cutting it for me anymore.

It was only in looking at a picture of me and my son taken at his first birthday party that it finally hit me like a brick falling out of the sky. It wasn't a bad photo; it was quite nice, really. But I lacked life in my eyes and the kids were in front of me, covering up my body. Sometimes I would lift my head up extra high in pictures so I wouldn't have a double chin. Double chins are, in my opinion, the worst afflictions known to mankind.

As I sat looking at my face, my body, my eyes in this picture, I realized once and for all that somehow it was time for change. The picture of myself represented my life and what I had allowed it to become. It was as if I was looking at a cart of apples, the apples being all the pieces of my life. Suddenly, the bottom apple was pulled and the rest of me came tumbling down. I had no choice but to take a good hard look at myself. In the back of my head I heard Obi-Wan Kenobi saying, "It is time Luke Skywalker," and knew with quiet certainty that something had to give.

Welcome To Our World

I was born the second of five children. My father was in the service and didn't get a chance to see me until a few months after I was born. In my baby book there's a telegram that says, "YOU ARE PROUD FATHER OF BABY GIRL SEVEN POUNDS THIRTEEN AND ONE HALF OUNCES. BOTH DOING FINE. CALL WITHIN SEVEN DAYS. CONGRATULATIONS LOVE MOTHER AND DAD." Seven pounds thirteen and one half ounces. That's an average weight for a baby, even by today's standards.

My Big Fat Head

I remember my childhood quite clearly, even if the years have altered the details a bit. It's like you swear your favorite toy was a red pickup truck, and you find out it was a blue pickup truck. It was still your favorite toy, even if you mistook one color for another.

A constant remark in my childhood was "what a big girl you are." Compared to my scrawny, finicky older sister I guess I was a big girl. Even back then I felt wide or thick when this comment was made as opposed to feeling taller and slimmer. I was an average, healthy child. My older sister was smaller and thinner. I was a good eater finishing every bite on my plate, never complaining about food. I didn't understand why my sister would sit looking at her plate commenting "yuck" over her food. My sister would eat lunch and a snack, then go out and play. I wanted more snack. And with this thought came a sense of shame, as if it wasn't normal to fantasize about food in this way.

As a small child and well into adulthood, I used to watch how other people ate. These memories are still prominent. For example, I was shocked when a cousin of mine ate a plain hot dog, passing on the condiments; my baby sister ate pickles sideways; my girlfriend mixed peanut butter, jelly and milk in her mouth before swallowing; and most of the neighborhood kids' favorite ice cream was that plastic cone shaped sherbet with a gum ball at the bottom from the ice cream truck. That's how I related to people, by the foods they liked. Just as certain songs bring back memories of times gone by, certain foods do likewise for me. I was compelled to watch others eat, see how they held their forks, picked up their food and chewed it. How much food did they scoop up at once, and, most important, how long were they able to wait between bites before picking up more food.

Now, if I derived amusement from life's little pleasures like watching people eat, you can only imagine what television commercials did for me! Forget the newest toys, did you see the double fudge, cream filled cookies they just came out with? Television land has an ingenious way of presenting cereal and snack commercials that are shown during

Saturday morning cartoons, and I was taken by each one of them. I was entranced by sugar cereals that were good for you because they also had fiber in them, gummy candies that were fat free, then you had chocolate milk, strawberry milk, pudding, jello, snack cakes…it boggled the mind. Where could I go to buy these things? I wanted them all and I wanted them NOW! Even if the food emitted a neutral feeling (like, say cheesecake), by the time I was done watching these kids say "Mmm, sooo good, I loovve cheesecake", I was hooked. I would sell my skinny, finicky older sister for one bite of that cheesecake! Lucky for me we lived below my father's parents and they would buy us just about anything. Ah, my grandparents, just the thought of them brings about warm fuzzy feelings of food!

Mangia, Mangia

My father's parents are typical Italians. They're fiercely loyal to their loved ones and would do anything for them. Their home and land are meticulously neat, and the best way they know how to show affection is by feeding you. My father was adopted into this Italian family at three weeks old. He looks Swedish or German with blond hair and blue eyes and grew up in a family where everyone has black hair all over their body and is named either Anthony or Mary.

My grandmother was so dedicated to keeping her home clean that a speck of dust didn't stand a chance. Grease or mildew had a life expectancy of about thirty seconds; the woman was a cleaner. I loved visiting my grandparents. We ate what we wanted, watched what we wanted on television, and were never forced to do anything other than lie on the sofa and eat. When we walked in the door Nonie would have a pasta dinner ready with all the fixings. "Mangia, mangia" she would say and my mouth abided. Immediately after dinner, she'd break out all the sweets she had (usually fresh from the bakery that morning). I was stuffed, but somehow always managed to eat dessert. I would unbutton my pants, take a deep breath, and eat on.

When I was 27, my grandmother died of diabetes mellitus. Too much sugar, and she never stopped eating it. Not even when she was really sick. She developed gangrene on her feet and suffered terribly. Her personality had deteriorated and the grandmother I had known and loved was forever gone. My grandmother not only passed on the message to me that food is love, she taught me to "skieve" things. This meant that some things were dirty: money, restaurants, and new clothes. If you touch money wash your hands because it's dirty, don't eat in the restaurants; they drop rolls on the floor and put them back in the basket, and possibly spit on your food, never wear new clothes without washing them first; dyes and germs. Much of my obsessive-compulsive behavior focuses around my grandmother's beliefs. My childhood consisted of a series of "Mangias" and "Skieve, skieve." I took her warnings literally and my big fat head absorbed and stored the information just so it could torture me for years to come. Her paranoia became my reality. As a side note, fat heads aren't dumb, but quite the contrary. They are cunning. They have the ability to bring your biggest fears forward and feed off them like a parasite.

My grandfather is a loud, boisterous man whose self-proclaimed favorite pastime is engaging in argumentative conversation or in his terms, "breaking balls". He, like my grandmother, spoiled us rotten. Most memories of my grandfather are food related. As children he used to take us to Dairy Queen not for an ice cream, but for a sundae. He saw nothing wrong with us eating a huge banana split and then asking for seconds. He believes that a four-year-old can and should devour a box of cookies at one sitting. One word my grandfather has a hard time comprehending is "moderation". I'm not even sure it exists in his vocabulary.

When my children were born my grandfather fed them as he had fed me, cookie after cookie after cookie. I would beg him not to give them any junk food or they would end up like me, struggling with weight issues all of their lives. And though the children had the smell of cookies on their breath with matching crumbs on their shirts, he denied giving them anything. He just couldn't help it. Love and food were one in the same. My children love to visit him; they get to take home candy bars, boxes of crackers, big bottles of juice and a half-gallon of ice cream. The minute my son walks in he makes a beeline for the candy bar drawer. My grandfather giggles, looks at my children with all the love in his heart and tells them to "Take five a piece."

Back To Being Four

Until I was seven years old my family of seven lived underneath my father's parents. I believe television commercials were what started me on my quest for food hits. By food hits I mean a 'hitting the spot' type of food. I would eat and eat waiting for something to hit the spot, like it did for those kids on the Saturday morning commercials. For instance, when you hear someone who just took a shot of Grand Marnier say, "Ah, that did it for me", that's the hit I mean. A warm, fuzzy relaxing whoosh right through your body, an "I really needed that" sensation. I was certain I would find that magical food or combination thereof that would satisfy my insatiable hunger. But nothing ever did, because it wasn't a physical hunger I needed to fill.

As a child I would overeat to pass the time, or from boredom, or because my favorite show was on and I wanted to snack through it. In the middle of a hot, humid afternoon when I had played all the games I could possibly think of, I would sit on my front porch and suddenly think that a fudgiscle might change the day. Eating provided a cushion of comfort I didn't get anywhere else.

Living with my grandparents was similar to living in Willy Wonka's kingdom. They bought enough junk to have stock in Hostess. I can't remember a time when they were without sugar snacks. Food was not a means to live, but an abused pastime. My mom constantly asked my grandparents to stop feeding us junk, but it was to no avail. They found ways to sneak us snacks. Imagine living in Willy Wonka's kingdom and having your parents tell you not to lick the wallpaper—impossible!

My Finicky Older Sister

My older sister Jewels was my closest companion from birth to early adolescence. Jewels was funny, quick-witted and had a retort for everything. She could negotiate her way past a pride of starving lions if she had to. From childhood through late adolescence I envied Jewels, (who is fifteen months my senior), to a point of despising her.

Jewels was toothpick skinny and picked at her food, never eating too much. She was popular, outgoing, and would participate in numerous activities with a confidence I wasn't born with. Our mutual friends were Jewels' age and every last one of them just happened to be skinny. These were one cookie type of gals, the kind that would rather play than eat. The kind who would suddenly say, "I'm starving, I haven't eaten all day." I happened to be over such a girl's house when her mom placed a fresh batch of chocolate chip cookies on the table. I was drooling at the thought of eating one when my friend, much to my surprise, said, "I'm not hungry—I don't feel like any." *Excuse me ?* Since when do you have to *feel* like a chocolate chip cookie to eat one? I couldn't understand how any child could refuse such temptation. I felt compelled to eat as much as possible until my stomach hurt. And most of the time, that's what I ended up doing.

When I was seven years old we left our cramped apartment for a large Victorian home twenty minutes north of Boston. I would be entering second grade in the fall of that year. The whole summer lay ahead to explore our new surroundings. My sister and I were allowed to go to the corner store and walk around the neighborhood. Frequently people would ask if we were twins, or assumed I was the oldest. We had the same haircuts, the same clothes and similar features. I didn't particularly care to be thought of as the oldest. I wanted to be small, petite, and hardly noticeable. But neither my love of food nor my gene pool would allow that to happen.

Corey

My baby sister is five years my junior. We shared the same room for a few years before either one of us entered adolescence. Corey was mouse quiet and timid. Her brown hair and deep brown eyes were unlike the blonde hair and blue eyes Jewels and I shared. Her shape was not like my solid even keeled body, nor was it like Jewel's skinny frame. Corey was thin, with long legs and a short waist.

Corey had the ability to be in a room unnoticed among her array of stuffed animals and Barbie dolls. Her appearance was disheveled and her hair was a matted mess behind her head because she wouldn't let my mother comb it. Most of Corey's time was spent drawing or playing alone with her many imaginary friends.

Corey ate finicky like Jewels, but didn't complain as much about the quality or quantity of the food. She ate with little bites and picky fingers. She would scrutinize her food, examining it for signs of abnormality. If she found something on her food she didn't care for, she'd grimace and begin to remove it with her picky fingers. Then she'd take 'sample' bites to ensure it was still a quality worthy of her eating. Corey, like Jewels, was thin throughout her school years. Not Jewels skinny, but thin enough. I was the only girl my parents had who didn't fit into normal sized clothing. I was the only girl who hated dressing for family functions because I was wearing what fit me and not what was necessarily in style. I was the only girl who always had to return pants bought at Christmas time.

Has Anyone Seen D.J.?

My youngest brother D.J., the baby of the family, was always missing. He had a habit of hiding in cubbyholes, behind bushes, under stairs, wherever he could fit. My mother would panic every time he went missing, and we'd have to go on a manhunt to find him. We'd go around in circles calling his name. D.J. never answered—not once. When you found him he usually smiled. Sometimes he fell asleep in his little cubbyhole under the hall stairs and didn't hear the commotion. Other times he just didn't want to respond. Upon seeing him my mother would put her hand to her chest and let out a big sigh. She was living on the edge with this little one. He was low maintenance as a brother but high maintenance as a son. I thought of D.J. as a cute baby whose head I would mindlessly pat as I walked by.

When D.J. was a teenager he began drinking a weight gain formula from a health food store designed to help build muscle. He also wanted to put on a few pounds. He would drink 2000 calories and then eat a full meal. He lifted weights religiously as part of this regiman. It took D.J. quite some time to put on weight. I was in awe that a blood relative of mine had to work just as hard to put the weight on as I was working to try and keep it off!

Maybe It's The Runs

I received my first menstrual period at eleven years old. For three whole days I mistook cramps to be the pains of diarrhea. After the third day of cramping and underwear changing I realized it might not be the runs after all. I asked my mother to come to the bathroom for verification purposes. You would've thought I won the lottery! She said, "congratulations, now you're a woman!" A woman?

That night my father came into my room and said, "Congratulations honey, I heard you got your period." If the god of lightning had been kind enough to strike me dead on the spot, I wouldn't have complained. To say I was embarrassed would clearly be an understatement. There I stood, newly showered in my flannel pajamas, wet combed back hair and standing in the middle of my room, for he caught me in mid stride to my desk. Frozen in my tracks and feeling the bulk of the giant maxi pad (which back then was like straddling a log), he congratulated me. I was mad at my mother, the informer. It was too embarrassing a topic, and one I didn't see the need he be aware of. My mom explained she told my father so that I wouldn't have to be uncomfortable if I were not feeling well due to my period. This way, she said, I could come right out and say, "Dad, I have my period, I'm not feeling well." I looked at her like she was crazy. Like that was *ever* going to happen!

After my initial period I began to gain noticeable weight. Until this time I may have been considered a bit 'pudgy', but certainly not heavy. I had stopped playing tag, jump rope, and hopscotch, activities that helped keep my weight in check. My sisters on the other hand, were still both skinny.

By age twelve I began smoking cigarettes, another addiction that proved bad for my health. Just as I ate too much, I smoked too much. One morning before school, I was sitting with a friend smoking a ciga-rette *knowing* I was cool when my brother Butchie drove by on his bike. I'll never forget the look on his face when he saw me smoking. I chased him down and made him promise not to tell my parents. Then I prom-ised him I would never smoke again. This seemed to satisfy him, and I sent him off to his side of the playground. Boy, I almost felt guilty, it was too easy to lie to my brother; he was a real softy.

Butchie Boy

I adored my brother when he was born. My mom said she was afraid that I would suffocate him because I was always climbing into the crib to hug and hold him. My brother Butchie and I share the most similarities out of all of my other siblings. We both had weight issues and the same fat heads. Throughout his childhood he would gain and lose weight going through periods of being thin and being heavy. He was three years my junior, and as long as I was the boss, we got along just fine.

My brother gained and lost weight depending on where he was in his life. If life was good, he was thin. If life was difficult, he was heavy. And when he was heavy, he was mean. He, like myself, developed other addictions and soon found himself in a state of spiritual bankruptcy. By this I mean he fell into a sort of Black Hole, a space that went so deep that it took him some time to recover from it.

Two years into his own recovery my brother called me after the birth of my third child to congratulate me. He told me that he had lost sixty pounds on a diet regimen and felt great. He also shared with me his life, something I hadn't heard about since our childhood. We had grown apart during the years and it was quite an amazing thing to get a connection back. If my brother or I weren't in some form of recovery from our fat heads, I'm sure neither one of us would have bothered with the other. You see, Butchie and I share the same frame of mind when we're overweight. We are unhappy, gloomy, and possess a 'no way out' attitude. When we're not bingeing the world is a nice place and problems are just problems, not catastrophes. It has taken us both a long time to realize that refraining from overeating was crucial to filling our voids. It was also crucial to ending the pain of our big fat heads and all the behaviors that result from its lardy goop.

Consider This

At thirteen years old I experienced a growth spurt. When Nonie commented I was getting thin I proceeded to eat four chocolate chip cookies in a row. I figured now that I was growing I would probably be 'naturally' thin. So why worry about a few cookies?

Growing up is awkward. The body begins to develop, you start to become attracted to the opposite sex, you think you're as wise or learned as any adult you know, and yet you still need the security of your teddy bear when the lights go out. The expectations of trying to keep up with other kids and fit into the norm are a struggle that begins when you're old enough to realize that society is divided as if we were all in different religious sects. From out of the blue it hits you that no, we can't all just get along. Where you once had five 'bestest' friends you now have three. The other two have moved into a different group and want nothing to do with the likes of you. You too, will leave a few friends behind for the benefit of moving up the social ladder of success. You watch as a sort of mixing and dumping roulette occurs. And it's partly because you're a preteen with little brain and surging hormones, and partly fear that if you screw up now your reputation is ruined for life, that you choose the group you want to be part of; then hope it wants *you* to be a part of it. You reluctantly dump your best friend whom you'll miss dearly to be part of a hierarchy from which you think you will benefit down the road. This continues through the years and materializes in the business world, in neighborhoods, in mother's groups, just about everywhere. And this is not the result of having a big fat head; this is life. Having a big fat head during these periods, however, does not help matters any.

At twelve and thirteen years old the most prominent emotions one has is where one fits in on the scale of popularity. At this age one doesn't mull over politics or cause and effect, or schoolwork. One thinks about friends and fitting in and feeling secure in an insecure environment. To preteens heading into full-blown teen hood, these are the politics to ponder. Picking the right group is essential for survival throughout the remainder of your school years. Fat or thin, smart or athletic, it doesn't matter. It's all in the group. You create your own reality by the choices you make. And believe it or not, these years can end up being the reason you get into therapy at age forty.

I tried to be everyone's friend, agreeing my way through school. Even if I didn't agree, I agreed. I secretly held extremely high expectations for myself, yet lacked the self-esteem necessary to fulfill my expectations. This left me with a sense of failure surpassing any successes I might have had. The result was an empty hole. I took every loss whether it was from a recreational sport or a board game as a personal attack on my character. Beginning at twelve and lasting into my twenties my life was one big identity crises. I couldn't describe my personality or my needs if I were asked to. When the bell rang after the final class, I couldn't wait to go home and hit the refrigerator. I substituted eating for feeling. It was so easy to eat away feelings. Just like drinking or getting high, it was a release.

Yer Out!

When I was fourteen years old I was expelled from a Catholic high school for the possession of narcotics. I was innocent, yet not. Anyway, I was forced to switch from an all girl Catholic school to a public junior high school mid semester. This was my first experience in a public school system and I was frightened of what would become of me. There were no uniforms, no nuns, different subjects, and worst of all, boys to distract one's attention. On my first day of school I wore a tight pair of Bonjour jeans I thought might make me look thin and a turquoise turtleneck. I had been in a school uniform for so long I wasn't even sure what was in style. I was relieved when the teacher seated me at the back of my homeroom. From there I could observe everyone, but they couldn't observe me.

My homeroom teacher was easy going, but he did not take public displays of affection lightly. Every day I would watch (kind of sideways with my eyes so not to be caught) a girl who was turned around in her seat talking to a cute guy. She was giggling and flirting and touching his face, leaning toward him to shower him with baby kisses. Her whisper was too soft for me to hear, but I could imagine by the boy's expression that it had a romantic undertone to it. I was fourteen years old, yet felt like a young child watching a television soap opera. The teacher would look at them disgusted and ask the girl to turn around in her chair. I would look at this cute guy and want so desperately to be that girl, that skinny, blonde haired girl with the dimples. At fifteen pounds over-weight and squeezing into a pair of tight jeans I wasn't even sure were in style, I was definitely not competition. I sat in the back of homeroom feeling extremely fat and self-conscious, thinking no boy in his right mind would ever like me.

Ninth grade was my last year of junior high school. I was grateful for only having to be the new kid for a short time. It felt like everyone except me had known each other for years and years. In high school three junior high schools were combined and everyone would have to adjust. This would even things out a bit.

My first day of high school did not go smoothly. I smoked pot before attending my tenth grade orientation. Sitting in homeroom and just about stoned to blindness I suddenly realized that I had sat in gum. I had on cream corduroys; the thick lined type. The gum was stuck between the lines of my pants like cement. The only parts of the day I can recall is trying not to trip in my new too high clogs and attempting unsuccessfully to peel this gum off my pants. Where my homeroom or any of my classes were, I couldn't tell you.

During my first year in high school I made a new best friend. We wore the same size clothes and bought the same jeans and shirts. I felt like I had a twin sister, someone special. My new best friend seemed to possess all the qualities I lacked. She could readily talk to boys and always had a boyfriend. I thought she was much prettier than myself and I wished I could have been more like her. I placed her on a pedestal along with my sister thinking her green grass must be nice.

My chameleon personality allowed me to be friends with any given group in high school. I can't say I belonged with a specific crowd and liked the fact that I could, at any given moment, blend in just about anywhere. I was, however, still overweight, insecure, and without a boyfriend. Not exactly items to die for on the "I must have" list when you're a teenager. I looked forward to the end of the day so I could walk home in peace. I enjoyed walking alone and thinking about the events of the day, embellishing, as I would have liked them to happen. I meandered slowly, fantasizing all the way home.

I used to fantasize about anything and everything that affected my life that I wanted to change but for some reason couldn't or wouldn't. It could have been as little as "I should've thanked so and so," to as big as "how could I have done such and such." I would go over the incident again and again adding different scenarios and imagining the new outcomes.

When my Irish grandfather died my fantasizing provided me with a defense for both denial and security. I fantasized he had to "disappear" because of a World War II secret he knew, and would be able to materialize again years later. This way I was able to keep him alive in my head forever, even though my heart knew different. And why did my grandfather have to go and die at a most crucial time in my life? He died on the weekend of my college excursion to Canada. My girlfriend was going to set me up with her boyfriend's friend and it was supposed to be a pretty promising weekend. Blacky (John Stamos) from General Hospital was going to be the special guest and would be signing autographs. And now I was going to miss it. On top of that, I had to contend with his death. What a curse to be fat and without a grandfather. What a curse it was indeed.

Pa

My Grandfather used to call himself the "handsome prince." He was generous, patient, and I worshipped him. He was the kind of person who would give you the shirt off his back, and never ask for anything in return.

When my grandfather retired he practically lived in the basement working with wood. In the evening you could barely hear the television over the hum of the radial arm saw. He made curio cabinets, mirrors, animal figurines, and pictures carved from wood. He once presented me with a picture of myself that he carved out of wood. Somehow the picture got lost. I remember my grandparents blaming my parents and my parents blaming my grandparents because no one could remember who had the picture last. He started to carve another picture, but didn't have a chance to finish it before he died. My picture was one of the last pieces my grandfather worked on. He had six other grandchildren and he picked me for his favorite. That was quite an honor in my family. I mourned the loss of the original picture, and always hoped that somehow, like him, it wouldn't really be gone, but would turn up later.

When I found out my grandfather had died, I thought I would be too sick to my stomach to eat. I assumed I wouldn't be able to eat for days. But not more than four hours after his death I found myself at Burger King ordering enough breakfast for 2 people. The food went down without a hitch. I felt guilty because even death couldn't stop me from eating. After the wake I stopped by Brigham's with my cousins for a large M&M chocolate sundae. It was fourteen years ago and I still remember the sense of satisfaction and relief that sundae brought me.

My grandfather was not an eater. He was a small man no taller than 5'7" and no heavier than 140 lbs. He would consume three square meals daily. Every night after dinner he would have dessert. His favorite dessert was a baked apple with vanilla ice cream on top. His second favorite dessert was a bowl of vanilla ice cream. He liked to have just 'a taste of something'. That's all his body or mind required. I enjoyed sleeping over my grandparents and spending time with my grandfather. He was far more patient with me than was my real dad.

How's Marlboro Country, Girls?

When he was thirty-five years old my father quit smoking. Life was easy for me before dad kicked the habit. When he stopped smoking his sense of smell was restored. I was fifteen years old and smoking on a daily basis. As my girlfriends and I breezed by my father reeking of cigarettes he would say, "How's Marlboro country girls?" just to let us know he knew. My girlfriends laughed, but I was embarrassed to be caught. I never knew what kind of mood my father would be in when I walked in the door. If he was in a good mood any little thing could set him off into a bad mood. If he was in a bad mood, I stayed away from him. Unfortunately, I was the one who usually swayed his moods.

My father was a much stricter disciplinarian than my mother. Our stubborn personalities did not mix well. I didn't like the idea of having to tell my father where I was going to be every minute of the evening and he didn't allow me to go out until I did so. Our relationship during my adolescence was full of turbulence and based on a battle of the wills.

On Saturday mornings my house would be echoing with the sounds of the Beatles or The Who, courtesy of Dad. I can't remember a Saturday when "Benny and the Jets" or "Tommy" didn't awaken me. My girlfriends loved to sleep over my house because of the easygoing environment. My friends considered my father 'cool' and a few girls had mentioned that they had a crush on my Dad. As a teenager I can say, this did not impress me. It more or less grossed me out!

My father was on the thin side and could eat as much as he wanted without gaining an ounce. In his mid-forties his eating behaviors finally caught up with him and he has gained and lost weight many times since. My father, unlike myself, prefers real food to junk food. He can easily overeat on a good meal, especially during the holidays. Our common bond pertaining to food is a problem with our shut-off valves. No buzzers sound and no lights go off to signal us that our stomachs are full, so we eat beyond full. My father claims he does not share the same feelings I have for food, but that he simply overeats because he doesn't watch his intake. I think he's just like me. I mean you don't just get a big fat head from nowhere, right?

Breathe, Kick, Wheeze

After my first diet failed at sixteen, (or I failed to do the diet) I decided that lack of exercise was the culprit for my weight problem. I was a good athlete as a child, but became self-conscious when I began to develop curves. I would sit on the sidelines in school longing to participate, but too afraid to be teased if something went wrong. What if I missed the ball? What if I tripped? I acted as if a tenth grade game was the World Series and it was resting on my shoulders. The thoughts swirled around my head like poison. I was better off regretting the fact that I could have been good, than to take the chance that I wasn't.

My mother taught yoga classes down the street at an all women's gym. She suggested I try one of the aerobic classes and if I liked it she would sign me up under her discount. I took one class and signed up at the gym. I purchased the latest fitness garb and walked around the gym in circles trying to decide what to do first. I had a choice of free weights, circuit trainers, or an aerobics class. I usually began with the aerobics class. My attempt to keep up with the instructor was hopeless. And how the heck did she consistently get her leg up to her ear?

The amount of exercise I could do was limited by my smoking. After fifteen minutes of aerobics I began to cough and wheeze. I'd have to stop and focus on my breathing; taking two shots of my inhaler. Back in the early 80s aerobics in a gym was more like doing one continuous jumping jack with different arm movements. It wasn't long before I quit taking aerobic classes. It was too confusing trying to keep up with the instructor's moves. This arm went here, that arm went there. I didn't realize losing weight would entail so much work!

After dropping the face-paced aerobics, I switched to weight machines and free weights. The total time I spent at the gym was an hour. The total workout time ranged from fifteen to thirty minutes. I thought stretching before and after exercise was a waste of time, so I faked it. Can you imagine faking stretching? I'd lie on the floor and if I thought someone was looking at me I'd give a little pull on my leg, like I was concentrating on this important move. Sit-ups were also faked. By the tenth sit up I was sprawled on the floor staring at the ceiling, my stomach in pain from the workout. As I lay on the floor I'd look around and admire all the thin bouncy girls and wonder where they got their energy. I'd listen to their conversations about how their weekends were, their boyfriends, their plans for the coming weekend. Tuning into this information was almost too torturous. Compare, crunch, and swallow. That pretty much summed it up.

Drink Me

I tried my mom's latest nutritional kick to help me lose weight faster. She had been doing it for a few months and had lost weight. The trick, she said, was in the vitamins. They helped to burn your metabolism. The way the plan worked was that I was supposed to drink an herbal protein drink for breakfast and lunch, and then eat a 'sensible' dinner. The drink was taken with lots of vitamins. Theoretically, this would satisfy me – theoretically. I guzzled down the drink and told myself I was stuffed. Mmm, what a lunch!

The problem with this diet was I couldn't wait to eat between these so-called 'meals'. It started innocently enough, by snacking on carrot sticks, fruit, and wheat crackers. Then, feeling deprived and starved, I went berserk. Nothing in the kitchen was safe. My 'sensible' dinner could've fed a six foot two hundred pound lumberjack. The protein drink did not prove a wise choice. Even if it did possess all the required nutrients for the day, there's no chewing action going on. There's no feeling of actually having eaten something. I gained five pounds in one week on the herbal protein drink diet. I blamed it on the drink, not the added bananas I threw in the drink, or the snacking I did between meals. What happened? Was I this *inept* that I just couldn't lose weight? As with everything else, the diet went to the wayside. It was too much effort. I wanted immediate gratification. Maybe I was just meant to be fat.

At this point, desperate times called for desperate measures. A couple of my girlfriends were doing the old 'binge and purge' to lose their weight. I thought I might try it myself. I quickly found out that I was not bulimia material. I went into the bathroom determined to throw up the food I had just eaten. I stuck my finger down my throat and gagged so badly that I got a stomachache. I then proceeded to gag with nausea for the next half-hour. I never did throw up and I never tried it again. Then I thought if I can't throw it up, I'd push it out. A brilliant mind at work! I got two chocolate flavored laxatives from my grandmother, drank a glass of hot prune juice and waited. In no time I was in the bathroom. I was also in writhing agony with stomach cramps and diarrhea. Next time around I halved the dosage, but this only gave me bad gas and cramps. I decided not to try laxatives again, either.

Pain was the motivator for my failure of vomiting and taking laxatives. Being twenty pounds overweight was livable, right? Oh, how I envied those bulimics who stuck to it. Life was so unfair!

While attempts at new diets were in progress, I was still enrolled at the all women's gym. How I envied all the thin girls working out. I'd look at them in amazement and wonder what their secret to thinness was. I assumed, as always, they were naturally thin and didn't have to worry about weight gain. I'd want to buy the same exercise clothes to see if maybe the secret was in the leotard. The fantasizing I did over these women reminded me of the fantasizing I did in high school.

You know the girls in high school I'm talking about—popular, thin, boyfriends to spare. I would take in every detail of their being, memorizing their expressions, and inhaling their perfumes. Searching for anything that would help me feel a part of them. There had to be some sort of secret to being thin, and I wanted in on it.

I stayed at the gym on and off for years, but still sought help elsewhere. When the toning machines were first introduced from Europe I jumped right on the bandwagon. All you had to do was lie there and let the machines twist and turn you while you magically lost inches without breaking a sweat. I think I was the only person who never lost more than five inches in three months on those friggin' machines. I then dabbled in cellulite creams, mud masks, toning creams, and seven-day diets. The seven-day diets seem a dangerous mystery to me. One day you eat all the fruit you want, but you eat fruit exclusively. The next day you eat all vegetables, and so on. I never got past day two. So I tried another seven-day diet. This diet combined weird combinations of foods such as hot dogs and black coffee, and tuna and eggs. My brother lost ten pounds on this bizarre diet. Again, I couldn't make it past day two. The bottom line was that I was meant to be heavy. Every effort to control my eating became less and less intense. My world became narrower and more meaningless with every bite of a brownie. If only I could be thin, then things would be different.

If Only

My life has been based on a series of If Only's. I believed that if only I could accomplish my obsession of the moment before I died, I'd be cured of all my worries in my life. Here is a list of some of my If Only's:

If only I can graduate from high school…

If only I had sex…

If only I found true love…

If only I got married…

If only I graduated from college…

If only I had kids…

If only I lost weight (this was an acute If Only)…

If only I could wear tube tops, two-pieces, and hip huggers…

If only I could have the confidence…

If only I were happy inside...

After each statement add, "before I died, then I will be happy." Each time one of my If Only's was achieved, I was still me. I was the exact same person who had always existed. Nothing had changed. There was no universal Band-Aid. I was in pursuit of that big moment, the one that would transform me forever into the person I'd always hoped to be. What a huge disappointment to find that one by one, nothing worked. What a mess, if only I didn't have to die all the time, then I'd be happy.

I'm Dying

I've managed to get through my whole life without a cold or a headache or a stomachache. I have, however, been plagued by brain and stomach tumors, cancer of the throat, ulcers, and other deadly afflictions I've barely escaped from. Hypochondria is another favorite of mine. Somewhere along the line my colds became rare viruses that only I could catch and would surely die from. That mosquito bite? Oh, it came from some country in Africa and carried a disease. Flew all the way over just to bite me on the ass, the bastard. I probably only have a few days to live. Thanks a lot, mosquito.

I could relate to a movie I watched called "Inner Space". Martin Short was going to the doctor's every time the littlest thing went wrong in his life. I laughed out loud recognizing myself in his character, knowing full well that he was being absurd. But knowing I was being absurd and controlling my thoughts were two separate things. Being the least bit ill became a major dilemma. Every little ache meant a possible brain tumor or embolism; every little pain meant an ulcer or internal bleeding. You name the symptom I gave it a disease. For every illness, I had a food remedy. The cures were chicken soup, ice cream frappes, toast, and chocolate (the latter being the most efficient cure all). The odd part about my neurosis was that I had never really suffered through anything too traumatic. It wasn't as if I had a baseline of a sick childhood to fall back on. This was just another way to sidetrack myself and avoid the real issues in my life, the number one issue being my body image.

Wedgie Trouble

I attended a local community college for one year after high school to try and improve my GPA. After that, if my grades allowed, my goal was to go to a private nursing school in Maine. I studied hard and was accepted into the nursing school. I couldn't wait to begin a new life. This would be my first time away from home and I was looking forward to becoming an independent.

My first year of nursing school was the most difficult year of my life, a complete disaster. As a matter of fact, if I were offered a million dollars to relive my first year in nursing school, I wouldn't take a cent of it, not one penny. And *that's* my final answer!

Nursing school was 2 1/2 hours north of my house. I wore the jeans I thought made me look thinnest with a blue sweater. As I put on my clothes I thought of how much weight I was going to lose at college. Without home cooked meals and so much studying to do, I would barely have time to eat. The college campus was overwhelmingly large. Everyone looked as nervous as I felt. I had been feeling crampy on the ride up, and went to the bathroom just to make sure that what I had hoped wasn't happening wasn't happening. It was happening. There was blood all over my jeans; the *only* jeans that could possibly make me look this thin. The pants that would deceive others into thinking I was of average weight were ruined. I put on a pair of skintight jeans and picked my wedge. My fat was hanging over the sides of my jeans. Frustration drowned me for allowing such a weight problem to happen.

Far And Away

Nursing school was another universe compared to community college. It was more like boot camp than college. My friends here were different from my friends at home. There didn't seem to be an abundance of overeaters. They appeared to eat normal portions of food, sometimes even skipping a meal to study or sleep. I, on the other hand, became increasingly aware of my eating behaviors. This awareness caused more shame and guilt, but I couldn't stop eating. My roommate told me to help myself to her homemade batch of butterscotch brownies. I'd sit at my desk praying for her to leave the room so that I could. I felt like a thief eating, and then trying to rearrange them so it appeared that I had taken only one or two.

Studying couldn't be accomplished without a steady supply of food. It was hard to study without my mind wandering to the vending machine or to my roommate's stash. If I didn't have any snacks with me, I obsessed about when I was going to take a break from studying and go to the vending machine. If I did have some snacks with me, I was too busy eating to study. My grades reflected this. I couldn't memorize information because my mind was clogged with sugary goop thoughts. I tried going to the library, but ended up having to sneak in chocolate just to survive an hour of studying.

In two months I had gained 22 pounds and I was already 30 pounds overweight. My jeans no longer fit me; they graduated from snug to tight to unbuttoned to unbuttoned and partially unzipped to unwearable. I lived in sweat pants and nurses' scrubs. I was always hungry, an insatiable hunger. The lardy goop had me believing that I needed a constant supply of food. Though I knew I had put weight on, I tried desperately to ignore the actual amount by never trying on my jeans or fitted shirts. Instead, I opted for the 'comfortable' look. I had one shirt that I did feel thin in and wore this shirt (literally) thin.

I ate every meal like it was my last. Wednesdays, or "hump day" was a good cafeteria day. The cafeteria menu read, "Hump day is hoagie day." I had no idea what a hoagie was, until I learned it was what I called a sub. I *loved* hoagie day! I wanted TEN hoagies, but usually settled for one and a half or two. I looked forward to each and every meal like a foreigner enchanted by the wonder of a new country. I ate fast with my usual five-second no-chew, swallow only gulp policy that I had mastered over the years. There were little to no boundaries around food, and excuses for eating were ample: A. I needed to keep up my strength, studying burned calories, B. eating helped me to stay awake, C. eating a chocolate bar relaxed me. I never stopped eating, except to take a puff from my cigarette or a puff from my inhaler.

My bad habits worsened in nursing school. Not only was my eating out of control, but my nails were now nubs and my smoking bordered on offensive. My hands had broken out from an allergic reaction to the powder inside the latex gloves, and the clothes I had worn to college were stuffed away in a basket at the bottom of my closet. Once in a while I would try them on only to find the button reached to the right side of my hip and the buttonhole reached to my left. Being of no use to me anymore, back they went into the basket.

Here I was, at least 150 miles from home with painfully swollen hands, bleeding cuticles, 20 extra pounds on top of the 30 I already carried, and self-inflicted asthma. Physically being in my own skin was a very uncomfortable feeling. This was definitely not how I had imagined college life.

My smoking habit paralleled the severity of my eating habits. I smoked almost two packs of cigarettes a day and could barely breathe when I got out of bed in the morning. With all the discomfort smoking caused, I never once thought of quitting. I didn't want the mental shame that eating caused, or the asthma from the cigarettes, but it was a trade off. I received momentary comfort for the asthma and the weight, and any comfort was better than none. So my vices won. With protruding stomach, double chin, and thighs rubbing together I lived each day intimately hating the person I looked like, not wanting to deal with the fact that I was the primary cause of my suffering. Food and a cigarette break became my main concern at clinical. I smoked without consideration of other's feelings never asking, "Will it bother you if I smoke", because I didn't want someone to reply, "Yes, it does." I ignored my roommate's waving away the thick smog when she entered our room. By this point, we had stopped being friends. We just weren't compatible.

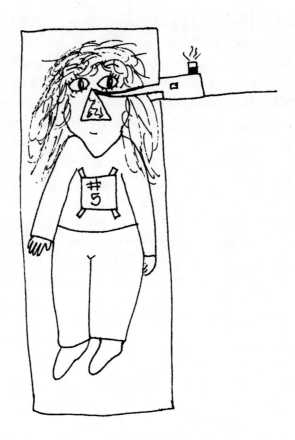

Quitting Time

In December my body finally quit on me and I suffered a serious asthma attack. I was in my dorm room in the middle of winter with a fan blowing in my face trying to get some air. I was taken to the hospital where I received two breathing treatments. Because the emergency room was extremely busy I was put in a hallway between treatments. It was as if I were a number, not a person. I felt exposed, alone and scared as I looked at the row of other people resting on their cold, steel tables. The medication wired me out, causing me to shake all over. I dozed on and off in a restless, wheezy sleep, feeling like Darth Vadar.

I was released the same night and taken back to the dorm by a girl-friend. I was feeling better, but was still having a lot of difficulty breathing. I woke up in the middle of the night choking and gasping and reaching for my inhaler. I couldn't wait until morning. I was fortunate enough to have the attack on a Thursday and my mom was driving up to take me home for the weekend so that I could rest. I wasn't allowed to smoke at home; maybe this would help me quit.

Just Like That

During spring break of my second semester at college my whole life changed; just like that. My mother, father and myself were driving down our street when a car hit us broadside. I was flung forward, hitting my face on the front seat. Other than feeling stunned and sore, I thought I was fine. At the emergency room I was given a muscle relaxant and was told to take it easy. A few days after the accident I woke with excruciating pain in my lower back and stomach. I had never experienced pain this bad and asked my parents to take me to the emergency room. The doctor on call diagnosed me as having a kidney infection. I was given more medication and sent home. I have to admit for the first time in a long time I didn't feel hypochondriac sick, I felt legitimately sick. The next few weeks were blurry. I suffered with crippling back pain, nausea, shakes, insomnia, and anxiety all day every day. Food was not my central focus. As a matter of fact, you couldn't get me to eat.

I returned to college still in severe back pain. My duties as a nursing student suffered. Two days a week we had what was called 'clinical' where we went to a hospital and cared for patients under the direction of our supervisor. The whole premise of clinical was to gain an experience of the hands-on work that being a nurse entails, such as lifting and transporting patients. The nursing instructors gave me small tasks, but I usually ended up sitting in a conference room doing workbook exercises.

Not soon after this, I went home. The pain was getting worse. I was having a hard time walking upright. This sheer misery couldn't be my imagination, could it? I told my college friends I would be back to visit them as soon as I felt up to driving. I told the nursing instructors that I was planning on coming back to complete my second semester of school. In a way I was relieved to be going home: my love life was non-existent, my nicotine and sugar consumption was out of control, and my grades reflected shades of mediocrity.

I became extremely depressed and began to lose weight. Food, my best friend, was now the enemy. I treated it as such by refusing to put anything in my mouth except water. In three weeks' time I had lost forty pounds. Eventually I allowed myself to eat two things: potato chips and grilled cheese. I considered these 'safe' foods.

When my back pain lessened, I returned to college and packed up my belongings. I realized it would be impossible to continue with my studies in my current state of physical and mental health. This was my easy out. Now I could return home the poor victim as opposed to the looser or quitter. At least that's what I could tell my friends. My goopy fat head however, told me I was a failure.

My college friends didn't recognize me when I walked into the cafeteria. They remarked on my weight loss and said I looked wonderful. As I received compliment after compliment I began to think this wasn't so bad after all. Who cared if I suffered and didn't eat; thin was not well, but it *was* thin. I bid farewell to my friends promising I'd return next year knowing in my heart I didn't intend to step one foot in this college ever again.

Getting Over The Hump

Back home I played the victim. I was plagued by anxiety, and didn't eat more than a bag of chips a day. My weekly visits to the doctor's showed one negative test result after another. My back pain was an enigma. My mother decided to send me to a psychologist who specialized in anxiety and panic disorders. He made copies of relaxation tapes for me and discussed ways to help me stop a panic attack that had already begun. When my panic attacks began to subside, my appetite returned. I was now eating a variety of foods, but still in small amounts.

In the meantime, my father had offered me a temporary job in Boston with good pay starting in September. I was learning to function with my back pain, accepting it as a normal part of the day. I was thinner than I had been in a long time, and was ready to move on and begin a new adventure.

Boston

The following September I began working in Boston. I bought a new wardrobe to go along with my new, thin self. I was down at least two dress sizes since the car accident. I confidently shook hands with my new coworkers and felt quite pretty in my brilliant blue knit dress. What a difference being thin makes! These people had no idea that just a few short months ago I was forty pounds heavier.

My coworkers were older, as in retirement age older. I decided it might be a long three months. We were taken up to the eleventh floor to a room with four desks. In the back of the room was a conference table filled with stacks and stacks of paper. Our job was to organize these stacks of paper, section by section. Boring didn't describe this job; agonizingly, mindlessly, tedious comes closer.

Lunch in Boston was like the Disney Land of food. Every corner had its own distinct odor of Italian, Chinese, or American cuisine. I ate at McDonald's every day. After lunch I would absorb myself in People magazine and obsess about the latest Hollywood hunk. My boring job only enhanced my fantasy mode. I imagined meeting celebrities and quickly becoming best friends with them, initiating my flight into stardom. I could fantasize for hours if I had to, and I *did* have to or else I might've been the first human being ever to die from boredom.

On my way back to work I passed a Mrs. Fields' cookie stand. It was not humanly possible for me to walk by without buying some cookies. Is Mrs. Fields the best or what? The cookies lasted as long as it took me to open the bag. If there was still time left on my lunch hour I'd go window-shopping, wondering why they didn't just use skeletons for mannequins.

Within a month of starting my job my clothes were too tight to wear. One month was a record for me. I had never gained weight this fast, and I was surprised to find that even my baggy dresses were becoming tight. It was this boring job that I thought would be a new beginning. All I did was eat and read. The only beginning this job gave me was an introduction to a fatter ass.

I purchased three large sweat suits of green, blue and gray and alternated wearing them. I convinced myself it was unnecessary to get dressed up for such a casual job. I had now gained twenty pounds in under two months' time. I guess my bout with anorexic eating was over. If it didn't try to walk off my plate, I ate it.

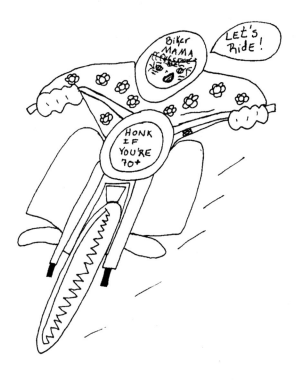

Ethel

While I was working in Boston I moved in with my Irish grand-mother, Ethel. Ethel is vivacious, funny and outgoing, but is a handicapped person who has no idea of her physical limitations. If she could, Ethel would be riding a Harley right now. Unfortunately she suffers from congestive heart failure, vertigo and diabetes. Though she wasn't heavy when I was a child, she did have an uncontrollable urge for the sweet. We share the same chocolate gene.

Ethel has been known to eat a box of fudge and then exclaim, "I didn't realize how much I was eating!" She recently graduated from borderline diabetic to a full-fledged diabetic, but still eats sugar consistently. She also searches the isles of grocery stores for sugar free cookies, pies, and candies. When she finds a new sugar free product, you'd think she won the lottery!

I can relate to my grandmother's search for sweetness, the never-ending quench for more. The one difference between Ethel and me is that she doesn't realize she consumes so much sugar, whereas I have always had an idea there was something wrong with the way I ate. Perhaps it was the difference in our body structure. If I were thin as a child and throughout my adulthood, as was Ethel, I wouldn't pay attention to the amount of chocolate I was consuming. It wouldn't make a difference if I ate one candy bar or ten. The only reason I did pay attention was because of the shame attached to the weight gain caused by the eating. Though Ethel may not see her addiction in me, I can clearly see my addiction in her.

To Eat Or To Study, That Is The Question

When the three-month position in Boston ended I moved back home and returned to college, this time in Boston. The advantage of going to a large-scale college is the garden variety of people a smaller college doesn't offer. You don't have to look at the same faces day in and day out for four years. Around every corner there's an opportunity to meet someone new. Not that I took advantage of such opportunities since I mostly kept to myself. However, I did feel better being an unknown college student among thousands than Jodi who lives in Purnell Hall, Room 2.

My performance at school remained mediocre. The large cafeteria where I ate lunch was loaded with goodies. As I ordered soup or a sandwich, I yearned to ask for one of every sweet that was available. Instead, I stuck to the inconspicuous vending machines. Two candy bars and a coke per study time were the usual. Study time lasted for an hour and a half. The candy lasted for five minutes, if I was lucky. I made sure I was in a closed cubicle of the library where no one could see me eating. Eating was such a shameful issue that it hurt to the core of my being. And I just couldn't figure out how to end this madness.

Towards the middle of the semester my back pain worsened. My anxiety level increased with the pain. During my menstrual period I suffered with severe cramping and nausea. Results from a gynecological exam showed I had a cyst on my left ovary that needed to be removed. At semester break my doctor would perform the operation. I was sure I was going to die on the operating table loveless, childless, and without a career.

Alive

I awoke to a nurse's voice in the recovery room. Blackness slowly filtered to colors and shapes. I was taken to a private room still groggy from the anesthesia. I opened my eyes and saw what appeared to be my mother's face hanging over the rails of the bed. She looked funny, like I was seeing her through an amusement park mirror where her face was extra big, especially her nose. She informed me I had been bleeding internally for close to a year. Without the surgery, I could have lost my life. This sobering news was blurted out by my anxious mother as I was just waking up from the anesthesia. I knew I was ill, but not that ill. The cause of my pain was a cyst that had ruptured a year ago and was left undetected. Bummer.

That day as I dozed in and out of reality, relatives sat vigil at my bedside. Among them was my Italian grandmother armed with Kleenex in one hand, and her rosary in her other. I had lost my right ovary and some of my left. But I was alive and felt good for the first time in a year. Even under anesthesia I felt my hormones had leveled out dramatically. The doctor's only concern was whether or not I could have children. Not that I had to worry about that any time soon, not a prospect in sight.

After surgery I allowed myself to eat as much as I wanted because I had the excuse of trying to keep up my strength. My friends came over with large frappes and ice cream. My bedroom was equipped with a couch, a telephone, and a television. I sat, queen of my castle, eating until I was uncomfortably full. There was no 'listen to your body'. I had no shut off valve. Nothing in me alerted me to the fact I should stop eating. So I didn't.

After I began to feel semi-recovered from the surgery I continued with my old life of school, food and isolation. I was convinced that I was either going to die an old maid or have to marry someone I didn't love. What I didn't know was that in just two short months my life would begin to change for the better.

Puppy Love

When I was eleven years old my parents rented a cottage in New Hampshire for two weeks in the summertime. They continued to rent the same cottage every year for the next six years. They packed up two weeks' worth of stuff for five children and a dog and drove two and half hours into New Hampshire listening to "Are we there yet's", and "I don't want to go's" the whole ride. The man who rented us the cottage was Dennis' cousin. Dennis' family lived in the cottage two doors down. I met him that first year and we immediately became good friends. We fished, hunted for crabs and frogs, walked in the woods, threw jack-knives at targets, walked into town, and swam all afternoon. New Hampshire smelled different than Boston. The air was fresh, we had a lake in our backyard and we brought along an overabundance of junk food given to us by our grandparents. What more could we ask for?

Jewels and I had a crush on Dennis' older cousin. Sometimes he and his friends would hang around with us, allowing us to wallow in our puppy love. No one seemed to notice I was pudgy, even in a bathing suit. Sometimes I'd wear a long tee shirt or a pair of shorts to camouflage my stomach. I could tell one of the boys had a crush on my sister. He treated her too nice, if you know what I mean. When a boy likes a girl the compliments flow, or he teases her, or goes out of his way to make her comfortable. That's what this boy did for Jewels. Toward the end of the two weeks Dennis' cousin came up to me and told me someone had a crush on me. My eyes bulged out and my heart pounded as I waited for him to say…"Dennis". *Dennis? He's a whole year younger than me, practically a baby!* Just then Dennis came walking towards me with a smile big enough to fill the lake we vacationed on. It was a cute smile that showed off his big white teeth and oozed with signs of puppy love.

I was disappointed that my knight in shining armor turned out to be this boy a *whole* year younger than I was. I mean, c'mon, he was ten and I was eleven.

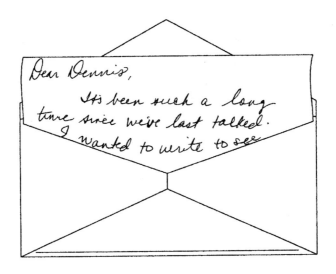

Dear Dennis,

It's been such a long time since we've last talked. I wanted to write to see

The End Of The Beginning

Working in Boston was so boring I had to create tasks for myself. I decided to write a couple of college friends I hadn't heard from in a while to see what they'd been up to. I also wrote Dennis. I hadn't heard from him in years and wondered how he was doing. What made me think of him and why I actually mailed the letter I'll never know. Fate is strange. Before I mailed the letter I decided I would not be disappointed if I didn't hear back from Dennis. This was just a letter from one friend to another, and nothing more.

One night after a movie I stopped by Ethel's house to see how she was doing. Ethel told me that Dennis had called earlier in the evening and left his number. I said, "Dennis who, I don't know any Dennis." I then asked her if she had gotten the name correct because Ethel tended to turn "Agnes" into "Gladys" and "David" into "Derek". She said she was sure of the name and told me she gave him my home number. Then she said, "You used to vacation with him." Immediately I knew who he was and realized it had taken him a long time to return my call.

Kismet

Dennis originally replied to my letter via the telephone in October of 1986. We discussed getting together, but nothing had materialized from our conversation. He told me he had a steady girlfriend of almost three years, and talked about his full time job. I suggested we all go out for dinner sometime and we both promised to keep in touch.

Now it was May of 1987 and I wondered why he was suddenly calling me. He informed me his girlfriend had broken up with him and he found my letter in his junk drawer. We decided to get together the following weekend. I hung up with a new excitement in my heart.

I dressed in a striped dungaree mini skirt and a tank top with a loose shirt over the tank that hung off one shoulder, the "Flash Dance" look. I thought I looked pretty good for someone who weighed 165 lbs. When the doorbell rang, I was putting away dishes. Not wanting to look too eager I asked my mother to answer the door. I heard them chatting and finally peered through the hall to see how he looked. I had no preconceived notion of what he was going to look like, and was pleasantly surprised when I first saw him. Dennis had grown to at least six feet tall. He was tan and wore a yellow shirt that was unbuttoned at the chest, the John Travolta look. When I saw those pearly whites of his I fell instantly in love right there in the doorway of my kitchen.

We walked around Boston, catching up on our lives. Dennis was clearly heartbroken over his recent breakup as he shared bits and pieces of his three-year relationship. Dinner was at my favorite restaurant. We ordered fried potato skins and chicken Parmesan. I enticed Dennis into trying the fried ice cream for dessert. He had never had it before and said it was tasty. I thought it was better than words. Before leaving Dennis promised to call me the following weekend. I made a mental note to cut down on my bingeing now that I had met the love of my life.

It Wasn't A dream

The week seemed to drag on and on. But on Friday, as promised, Dennis called. He wondered if he could come down on Sunday. It wasn't a dream after all; life was looking up! Every Sunday for the next few weeks Dennis would visit. We'd go out to eat and take long walks with each other. I liked this new experience of feeling comfortable around a man. Dennis was familiar to me, as if we had always been together. We did spend a lot of time with each other growing up, but it was more than that. It's like when you get a new piece of furniture and it already feels broken in. Like it was made just for you. That's how I felt about Dennis. He was my soul mate.

A first kiss with someone you are madly in love with is so magical you never forget it. It was a bit chilly out and his lips were comfortably cool. When they touched my own lips they felt like a soft, gentle sponge wiping at my mouth. I swear I saw stars, I saw rockets, I saw the Almighty God himself! And He was happy for me! I watched my boyfriend, a man who had always carried feelings for me in his heart, walk to his truck to go home. He was beyond handsome. He was perfect, and he was mine. I smiled for two days straight thinking of that kiss. And what a storybook romance I had fallen into; boy meets girl at ten years old and loves her forever. What could possibly measure up to that?

At Christmas I received gold earrings from Dennis. I couldn't wait for the next holiday-Valentine's Day. This was the one holiday I had always felt forgotten. Christmas and other holidays were easy to sneak by without a significant other, but not having a sweetheart on Valentine's Day was a toughie. I would finally get a big heart decorated with ribbons filled with luscious chocolates from my boyfriend!

Valentine's Day was finally here and I could barely wait for the evening to come. I didn't eat any chocolate that day so I could save my appetite for my special box of chocolate from my sweetheart. Dennis wished me a Happy Valentine's Day and handed me a mug, a stuffed animal, a pair of socks with hearts all over them, and a balloon. He told me he thought he'd give me something different, because everyone gets chocolate. The thought was precious, but I didn't want different, I *wanted* my chocolate. I actually asked him where my heart was. When he told me he didn't get me one, well, let's just say all those years of repressed emotions hit the poor guy square in the face. Dennis brought me a heart the next day. I felt embarrassed that my very first Valentine's Day was to be remembered by my taking a fit over a chocolate heart. Truth is, I still have the socks, the bear and the mug, so I guess his original purchase was the better choice.

Dennis and I dated for one and half years before he proposed to me on Christmas Eve 1988. We decided to get married in June of 1990. I chose a date and promised myself I would definitely lose weight for my wedding.

In April of 1989, my grandfather's tenants moved out leaving the downstairs apartment vacant. On a visit to their house I found myself walking around the apartment wishing I could afford to live there. I was going to school part-time and worked full-time as a receptionist. I threw the idea around to my grandparents and within a week the apartment was mine. After two months of driving back and forth, Dennis moved in with me permanently. This was a good move, I thought to myself as I started to cook dinner. I could buy what I wanted, eat what I wanted and do what I wanted in privacy. I should still cut down though. I'm getting married soon.

I worked during the day and took two courses at night for the next year and a half. Dennis worked during the day and joined a local gym where he faithfully worked out in the evenings. When I got home from work or school I would cook dinner. Then I would sit on my couch and eat watching whatever sitcom happened to be on. Dennis would come home from the gym happy, smiling and built. Damn, he looked good and I looked like shit. I had a hard time recognizing the emotions when I looked at his slim figure. I was jealous of his physique. Looking at him reminded me of what I wasn't.

It was still Willy Wonka land at my grandparent's house. They'd buy ten packages of cookies on sale and try to force feed you package after package. I would go down to the cellar where they had the goodies stored on shelves and pretend I was doing the laundry. I would then pull up a chair, flip through a magazine and eat. I continued living in the vending machines at school and work. My fifteen-minute break meant food. My hour lunch meant food. Everything meant food.

Ba-Bum-Ba-Ba, Ba-Bum-Ba-Ba

My wedding was not my wedding—it was my mother's. She booked the hall, mapped out the seating arrangements, handled the invitations, chose the hor'derves, and picked out my dress. Frankly, I was glad to let her take on the job. As a matter of fact, I relinquished all responsibility. I just wanted to get married.

My maid of honor and my bride's maids gave me a traditional bridal shower. It wasn't a surprise because Dennis broke under the pressure and told me about it. He initially told me we were going to a banquet for his friend. I asked him all sorts of questions, needing to know the exact details. I told him I had nothing to wear (at least not anything that would 'make' me look thin). I actually believed that certain outfits had the ability to transform me into something I wasn't. I call it 'The Cinderella syndrome'. When I found out the party was for me, I ran out and got a matching shirt and skirt outfit. I chose an outfit that fit. When you are heavy, there is no choice of outfits; there is only what looks best. A heavy person will spend an inordinate amount of money just to look slimmer even if the outfit is something that is not to their taste, or if the outfit will only be worn once. My personal style back then was the looking-slimmer style.

Party favors were tactfully arranged throughout the room. Someone placed a table along a wall and lined up all of my gifts. I assumed it was my mother. She couldn't have anything less than perfect when it came to preparing any sort of event, or she'd suffer with the feeling of imperfection, which was then imposed upon us in the form of a bad mood.

Mom

Being a mother is the most important job that exists. No one can replace the love a mother gives, and nothing can take away the pain that losing a mother causes. A mother is looked to for nurturing, comfort, advice and acceptance. Being a mother myself I have come to learn the irreversible effects, both positive and negative, that mothers have on their children.

I've learned that it's not so much the big stuff that hurts a child; it's the little stuff. It's the nitpicking (your hair looks awful, fix yourself up, are you going to wear that), the manipulating (do what you want to, but *remember, I told you so…*), and the feeling that no matter what, your mom has something to add to work you considered flawless. For example, your perfect picture? Giraffes *aren't blue silly*; they're yellow. Your 88 on the test? Too bad it wasn't a 90, just missed it by two points. What is meant to be constructive criticism for self-improvement turns out to be a stifling of your own creativity and talent that you assumed was fine and needed no improvement. However, here is your mom saying otherwise. At 30, 40, and 50 years old, a woman still wants her mommy to say, "I love your stick figure drawing. I love *you* for drawing it." Even if it was the worst drawing in the whole world. A child doesn't want a mom's criticism; criticism is easy enough to come by via other channels. All a child wants is approval, plain and simple. A mother's acceptance, for some, can be imperative to one's survival.

I have two friends who lost their own mothers at young ages. One told me that even if you don't get along, or you believe your mother's advice is manipulative, you still have her around. If you think you can't stand being in the same room with her for more than five minutes, count your blessings she's alive. And even if you call her for advice knowing it's a set up and she's not going to tell you what you want to hear, you still have the option to call. My mother is the only person on this earth whose opinion I take to heart. For this I have to be careful what I disclose to her. I don't think she, as a mother, realizes the god-like impact a mother has on a child. I say this because until recently I didn't realize this myself. And though realized, this impact for some reason is easy to forget since we, as mothers, do not consider ourselves gods.

My mother is a woman who had five children by the time she was twenty-eight years old. She was a loving mother who sang nursery rhymes and read books. I can still remember her singing "Three little ducks" and reading chapters of "Bed Knobs and Broomsticks" before bedtime. I basked in the beauty of her long red hair and big brown eyes. She wasn't a strict mother, and rarely followed through on her many threats that if we didn't pick up our toys today they'd be in the trash tomorrow.

When my mother was twenty-five years old she began taking yoga classes. This eventually led to her becoming a certified yoga instructor. Yoga was mom's escape from her everyday life. In the late seventies my mother drove the five of us to a children's yoga camp that taught the fundamentals of Jainism, a religion from India. This religion, from what I understand, bases its belief on the theory of preventing one's sins from a past life to follow you into this life via karma. Jainism concerns itself with the human soul and the universe's purpose for the soul. The goal is to achieve a state of Nirvana through moral discipline and the practice of ahimsa (non-violence), thus eliminating attachments and ignorance.

We stayed at the camp for one month. It was a peaceful, magical place. Children's lessons were taught in the morning and group chanting was in the evening. I learned about auras, meditation, and chanting. Everyone seemed to get along quite nicely in the commune-like environment. There was no arguing over nonexistent things such as the television or the phone. Located in the boondocks of New York, the real world seemed miles and miles away. Just being there was surreal: Gurus in white cotton clothing with long white hair and beards, chanting in a dimmed room with incense burning, the sound of chanting followed by the united hum of the Om sound. It was a spiritually swathing experience.

When I returned to the real world I continued to use these techniques, but on a much smaller scale. Today's therapists hand out tapes on the same relaxation and breathing procedures I learned about at camp. The process is to learn how to control the breath, thereby controlling the mind. If the body is relaxed, the mind cannot be in stress, and vice versa. Back home the techniques were still in my mind, but they came in second to smoking and eating junk food. Nothing can cure an addictive behavior if the addiction is not recognized. And my addiction was not yet in full bloom.

I remember my mother in two phases. As a young child she was constantly around and always available. If I needed her for any reason all I had to do was yell, "mommy" and she'd appear. When I was a teenager and she was involved in yoga, I didn't feel that she was available on an emotional level, at least not the way I wanted her to be. She was home, but more involved in her own life, developing a separate independence from her usual status as mother. Her friends would come over and they would practice yoga or other forms of healing. This was a painful experience for someone who selfishly wanted, and by this time was used to, having her mother all to herself.

My mom can fix almost anything. She is Martha Stewart meets Buddha meets the Victory Garden. Her persona for the most part is calming and warm to the touch, but at other times she can be like me. I don't exude calm. I would describe my energy as erratic. I *can* be calm and serene with practice, but mostly I give off shock energy—the kind you feel when you rub a balloon to your head and then touch someone.

My mother's eating patterns were not like mine, but were also poor. She was not overweight as a child or as an adult. She had a bad habit of not eating until two in the afternoon and then wondering why she felt so low on energy. She usually gives one of two excuses for this eating pattern: (1) I didn't realize it was so late, I forgot to eat, (2) I didn't have time to eat until now.

O.k., I cannot *possibly* understand this. I could always find the time to eat and *never* could I say there was a time I actually *forgot* to eat. The part of my brain that carries this type of information either got damaged or left out from birth because this kind of logic completely escapes me!

Over the past few years my mom's eating behaviors have changed for the better. She thinks its all the multivitamins or the special tablets that are supposed to keep you healthy. But I think it's the fact that she makes better food choices and eats at regular intervals.

My parents sold my childhood house and moved one hour north when my daughter was born. I don't see my mom as much as I'd like and when I do it's usually rushed and busy. When she drives down to visit she usually has three or four people on her list and spends a limited time at each place. Because of this, I often find myself competing with my own children for her attention, telling them to be quiet or becoming aggravated when they intrude on the conversation. She continues to be involved in her yoga and other non-mommy aspects of her life.

Although I am a grown woman with a family of my own, I will always want my four-year old mommy. The one who made me feel secure in an insecure world with her warm soothing touch. The one who, when she hugged me, made me feel so utterly safe and protected that nothing could harm me. The one who not so much told me, but showed me through her own path, that it was o.k. to be different. I miss the secure and safe feeling that she provided. I selfishly still want all her attention and mostly, her genuine approval. I can't help it. I so enjoyed my mommy when I was little. That's what happens when you're a good mommy.

I Do

Walking down the aisle was the only hard part of getting married. The rest of the service went quite nicely. I was calm, cool and collected throughout the ceremony. Dennis was sweating so badly I could see it dripping off his face. His brother and my sister were also very hot. Maybe all these layers of spandex-like material sucking my body in worked as a cooling device. It was June and had to be seventy-five degrees and yet I was cool as a cucumber. Go figure.

I was determined to participate in the chicken dance at my reception. After dinner mom suggested I circulate from table to table. I spent the next two hours circulating. By the time I finished I had missed most of the dances, including the chicken dance. I was angry with myself for listening to my mother. When I told her I felt like I had missed most of the dancing she told me that I didn't need to do *all* the circulating at once. But that was how my head worked, all or nothing, black or white, not one slice, the whole pie. When would these people in my life start to understand my logic? When would *they* 'get' it?

We chose Disney World for our honeymoon. Before boarding the plane I took two anti-anxiety pills and hoped we wouldn't crash and ruin my newly perfect life. The plane provided a movie, "Driving Miss Daisy", a grateful distraction. My husband opted to look out the window and "ooh and ahh" at the far away land below. The anti-anxiety medication was working. I sat back in my chair, absorbed myself in the movie, and tried to forget we were 35,000 feet in the air. I rarely turned my head and did not get up once, not even when nature called.

We were transported from place to place until we reached our hotel. Everything looked beautiful and fresh. My husband and I could barely contain our excitement. I tried to shake the feeling that some unknown person was going to come up behind me, tap me on the shoulder, and say, "just kidding".

Our hotel room came equipped with a small refrigerator filled with food. What do you think I did the second I walked into the room? I headed toward that refrigerator and gazed starry-eyed inside. It contained candy bars, cocktails, baby condiments, and water. I was about to take a box of M&M's when Dennis said, "Kid, it costs $4 for a box of M&M's; wait until we get to a store." Damn him, that wasn't the point! I wanted those M&M's and I wanted them NOW! So I said, "It's our honeymoon, what does it matter", in that sniveling I'm not worth the $4 voice. He replied, "I don't care what you do, it's just ridiculous to pay that much for M&M's." He was right. I put the box back and only resented him for about twenty minutes. We left the hotel and were off to Sea World where I was sure to find a box of M&M's or a good substitute. Food looked better, tasted better, and smelled better in the magical world of Disney.

I've Been Hoofed!

Dennis and I traveled to an animal farm located in the Disney
Kingdom. We have pictures of each other holding baby goats and
feeding the animals. We were given ice cream cones filled with whatever
it is goats eat. I was feeding a baby goat when an older goat, quite a
pushy character, jumped on my leg with force, digging her hoof into
me. Dennis got a picture of it. My face was distorted in pain, but the
picture itself turned out funny. Of all the people to jump on, the damn
goat picked me, the most self-conscious girl in the world.

I had a large bruise on my leg where the goat's hoof had landed.
Because I didn't want any attention drawn to me, I acted like it was no
big deal. It hurt like hell for at least twenty minutes and was sore for a
day or two. The thought of someone looking at my thigh to see the

bruise was unacceptable. I was sure the only thing they'd see would be the size of my leg. Perhaps they'd say, "Got enough fat on ya to protect ya from harm, m'am." Dennis couldn't stop his muffled snickering. He said, "Kid, I've never seen a goat do that to anyone." The goat basically attacked me for the food. Can't say I blame her.

No, You Go Ahead

Dennis asked me if I wanted to go to the whirlpool and relax. I told him I didn't feel like it, but he should go if he really wanted. This was the moment I'd been waiting for. No sooner did his elevator door close than I pressed the down button on another elevator. I had been passing this gourmet pastry shop all week in the lobby. I walked into the shop. It was vacant, which was good, real good. The girl behind the counter was pleasingly plump. We chatted and laughed and I ordered one piece each of six different cakes. I took the elevator up to my hotel room with a giant stack of Styrofoam in my hands and closed the door behind me. I ate each piece quickly, all the while looking over my shoulder for Dennis. I couldn't erase the thought that I chose cake on my honeymoon over a whirlpool with my husband. It's hard to admit, but the cakes were the more appealing choice. Chocolate torte, cheese-cake, marshmallow filled; I was in heaven.

When Dennis got back he found me moaning belly up in bed with crumbs and plates all around me. I looked over at him and said, "I saved you a lemon square." He scanned the room, and slowly shook his head. He said he had been in the whirlpool when two girls in bikinis came and sat on either side of him. He was down there scared to death I was going to come and accuse him of something or other. He was right. If I had eaten all that cake and then managed to waddle down to the whirlpool only to find my new husband sitting between two skinny girls in bikinis the poor bas-tard would've fried. What *had* he gotten himself into?

It Doesn't Change A Thing

Being married to Dennis paralleled living with Dennis. He was an easygoing, low maintenance guy. Cooking dinner was my job. I bought four pounds of steak and cooked the whole package. Then I would fry some onions and potatoes or boil pasta with tomato sauce. No vegetables were cooked. If Dennis took seconds before I was finished with my firsts, I eyeballed him so he wouldn't take too much. If I finished before Dennis, I had no consideration for him; I piled as much food on my plate as I could. All our meals were like this. I cooked enough food for four people and we usually ate alone.

Every morning I'd wake up with a sore stomach and nausea. To quell the nausea I drank a cup of coffee and ate a large muffin or bagel. Looking back at my morning nausea reminds me of what I had heard about alcoholic behavior. If you had a drink of alcohol first thing in the morning you wouldn't get a hangover. That's what I did with food. By ten o'clock I was at the vending machines buying cheese and crackers or cookies. I never exercised. My day consisted of going to work, coming home, eating, and going to bed.

My back had gone out earlier that year and continued to bother me. I went to physical therapy, but nothing helped. I was given painkillers for the soreness. After a couple of months, the doctor stopped prescribing the back medication. I was furious. He told me if I was in as much pain as I said I was he wanted me to consider surgery. I declined. I knew the problem was forty pounds of fat, no exercise, and an unhealthy diet. Being married hadn't changed a thing. It was becoming painfully clear that no one person could change me. With all my complaints of misery, with all the food sneaking, all my fantasizing, I considered myself as happy as I was ever going to be; I had settled. I hadn't known any other life beside one that revolved around food. I blamed all my problems on food. My back hurt, and I blamed it on food. I figured taking a pill would be easier than changing my life. And it was.

It's Because I'm Fat

I was doing the usual droning on about this one and that one, how my life seemed to be everyone else's fault when my friend suggested a twelve-step anonymous program that I might find useful. I had never heard of it before, but was willing to try anything. I looked up the program in the yellow pages, made a few phone calls, and went to a meeting. After three months in the program I had lost forty pounds. It wasn't as easy as it sounds. The food plan called for cutting out sugar and flour from my diet, eating three meals a day, and weighing all the food I ate. I was quite proud of myself. For the first time in my entire life I was the correct weight!

That Thanksgiving while everyone ate cookies and pie I ate my apple. What I didn't like about my new food plan was the sense of feeling left out. I was used to being the one who made the fun, fattening desserts and talked about how the diet started 'tomorrow'. Have you ever noticed that food is used as the main topic of communication on the holidays? "This is so good, that tastes delicious, wait'll you try one of these." And if you refuse dessert some people just won't take no for an answer. They continually ask, "Are you sure, are you sure?" at five-second intervals. I had nothing to talk about, but decided I'd rather feel left out on a conversation than to be fat.

Intermission

During 1990-1994 I was pregnant three times. I had one miscarriage and two successful pregnancies that yielded one beautiful daughter and one wonderful son. I left the twelve-step program with my first pregnancy, deciding I wanted to eat flour and sugar with my pregnancies. As a result I gained a good amount of weight all three times. Even with the miscarriage I gained thirteen pounds in four months. With my second pregnancy I gained forty-two pounds and with my third I gained thirty pounds, which wasn't bad, but it was a complete sugar diet. Nutritionally, I could've done better.

My Panic Attacks

My panic attacks seem to have correlated with my eating behaviors. When my eating climaxed so did the attacks. When I watched my diet, my attacks decreased. They began when I was fifteen years old and have followed me throughout my life like the plague. They occur with stress or excitement or with the end of something (death, or a season change) or the beginning of something (such as starting school).

The way I see it, we all have our problems. We just call them different things.

I'm termed (medically speaking) with having generalized anxiety disorder with obsessive-compulsive tendencies that will cause, during periods of high stress, severe panic attacks. The obsessive-compulsive behavior affects my thinking in a way where I have to pick *the* perfect bar of soap, *the* perfect aspirin, *the* perfect magazine, which incidentally, is *never* the one on top. The childhood game 'don't step on a crack, you'll break your mother's back' left me avoiding cracks for years for fear I really had that kind of power.

The attacks felt physical as well as mental. Mentally my mind raced, and I couldn't complete a thought. Physically I became over sensitized to every inch of my body. My body ached, my chest hurt, there was a lump in my throat, and my legs felt like jello. My vision blurred, my hands shook, and my breathing became erratic. I would hyperventilate and get numb tingly lips and fingertips. It felt as if I were gasping for air and couldn't get any unless I was in front of an air conditioner. I felt like I had to run from something at that very minute, escape as if in imminent danger. I frantically searched my mind for the reason of the attack, but could do nothing to stop it.

Sometimes I would have four panic attacks in one day, leaving me exhausted and depressed. An attack would last anywhere from five to thirty minutes, and once it subsided I'd need another thirty minutes to recuperate. Waking up in the middle of the night in a deep sweat with my heart beating out of my chest was the worst. I'd be shaking all over, afraid to fall back to sleep.

What my bingeing has to do with the panic attacks is both chemical and emotional. The more sugar I ingested, the more revved up my body physically became. After the let down of the sugar rush the shame would kick in, filling me up faster than the food. With the shame came the realization of what I had done to myself by gorging down food. Enter the panic attacks. I would begin one of my diets that would last no longer than one month. Once I lost five or more pounds, I was back to eating as much as I wanted. Hence the vicious cycle.

As I've said before, I'm not original. We all know people who obsessively clean their houses, or grooms their kids to perfection, or continually buy things then return them because the item at hand didn't satisfy in that 'ah' sort of way, or exercise until their joints need some kind of therapy. When I was a child I was carefree, happy and adventurous. As I grew older the carefree and adventurous pieces of me got replaced by the fears and expectations that go along with growing up. After that I became an adventurer only in my mind, between my ears.

Books And Addiction

We are given diets to follow and told to control our intake. Control our intake? How can an addict be in control? How can an addict eat in moderation? If I take a pill and have an adverse reaction, I know not to take the pill again. If I eat sugar and grow moody and irritable, or want more and more so I 'can't stop', it's considered a control issue. If something chemical occurs in my body that changes the way I think and feel over a period of time, if my mood is altered in any way after eating sugar, then I consider that beyond a control issue. I consider it an inappropriate response by my body that I can't control.

Some books on the market targeting wellness suggest increasing raw foods, brown rice, soybeans, and legumes, to name just a few. They say to stay away from a diet high in wheat, dairy, sugar, and carbohydrates. The market is saturated with these kinds of books. There are also books that say to get rid of all carbohydrates, or books that say a diet high in protein is the best, or less animal protein and more protein from legumes is the way to end the battle of the bulge. These books are all informative, and I'm sure they are all sufficient for a weight loss regimen. But for addicts a book is useless, unless there is a support system to back them up. Until I started to pay attention to my own instincts I wasn't aware of the extent to which food could harm or heal a person. What I am trying to say is that although correct in theory, the books don't matter when you are alone in your house craving a candy bar. The book may suggest eating this or that to combat the craving, but who cares? You're alone, no one's watching, and you can start again tomorrow. An addiction is an addiction is an addiction. Period. If you eat sugar in moderation but then slip or struggle, perhaps it is the sugar. Most won't admit such problems exist. Why? Because sugar is fun, sugar is satisfying, and sugar is sweet. No one quits doing what he or she loves even if it harms him or her without having to reach some sort of a bottom. Why should food be any different?

Full Circle

Holidays came and went and desserts were cooked, and I ate. I ate and ate and ate. I wondered why I couldn't lose weight and ate. I began to look forward to the next holiday just so I could bake up some concoction for the family. Who was I kidding? It wasn't for the family it was for me. It was always for me. If it had to do with sugar, it was personal. I knew it, my family knew it, and even my kids were beginning to realize that "This is mommy's ice cream." Which brings me full circle to where I began. A housewife with a hardworking husband who loved her, two beautiful children who loved her, and no stresses to speak of, from work or any other force in the universe.

I was sick of buying new clothes every time a holiday or event came along so I could 'hide' my fat better. My husband was sick of hearing me whine about having to go to these events. Most of all I was sick of my anxiety and panic attacks, which seemed to increase whenever I would binge. I was tired of my obsessive-compulsive rituals to which I'd been a slave to all these years. What was I going to do? Who could I turn to? This bingeing and obsessing over food was a serious problem. Society only seemed concerned if you were anorexic, bulimic, or grossly overweight, and even these people could easily slip through the medical cracks. No one worries about the average sized girl who can't get that brownie out of her mind, or the rigid dieters who constantly eat like birds to maintain a normal weight. If you look normal, you *are* normal, according to society. Any confession otherwise is an embarrassment and a porthole to self-exposure. Diet shops will give you diets to follow, but what good is it? What do you do when the diet is over? No one had ever told me I was not alone, that other people who are thin, average, or above average in weight had eating behaviors similar to my own. It wasn't as if I polled people and asked them if they binged and, by the way, how's their big fat head today?

Recovery

Back To What Worked

As I said before, my son was a year old and I was looking at his birth-day picture. I was pretending to like myself, pretending to be happy. I was struggling with where to turn for help when I remembered the twelve-step program where I'd lost forty pounds when I first got married. The support of the other members and the ease at which everyone discussed their eating problems remained embedded in my memory. I decided to return and give this program a second chance. I didn't plan on staying any longer than it took to lose this blasted twenty pounds.

Eliminating flour and sugar from my diet, I lost twenty pounds in two months. This time around, however, I didn't leave when I lost the weight. I found a place where people understood me as a whole person: the person of the general public, the mother, the wife, the neighbor, the friend, and the person who hid her true identity from the rest of the world. I could safely share all my identities with this group *and* stay thin, what a life! They understood my need to fill myself up with substance, to thicken my body with fat. My story was their stories. Stories of how one cookie turned into the whole package, stories of low self-esteem and the all-consuming devil of life itself: fear. People of different social and economic statuses, different races, and different sexes came together to share one common bond – the desire to stop abusing food.

The program itself was based on the belief that if you worked the twelve-steps you could maintain abstinence from compulsive overeating. The food program borrowed its twelve-steps from the twelve-steps of Alcoholics Anonymous:

1. We admitted we were powerless over alcohol, that our lives had become unmanageable.
2. Came to believe that a Power greater than ourselves could restore us to sanity.
3. Made a decision to turn our will and our lives over to the care of God as we understood Him.
4. Made a searching and fearless moral inventory of ourselves.
5. Admitted to God, to ourselves, and to another human being the exact nature of our wrongs.
6. Were entirely ready to have God remove all these defects of character.
7. Humbly asked Him to remove our shortcomings.
8. Made a list of all persons we had harmed, and became willing to make amends to them all.

9. Made direct amends whenever possible, except when to do so would injure them or others.
10. Continued to take personal inventory and when we were wrong promptly admitted it.
11. Sought through prayer and meditation to improve our conscious contact with God as we understood Him, praying only for knowledge of His will for us and the power to carry that out.
12. Having had a spiritual awakening as a result of these steps, we tried to carry this message to alcoholics, and to practice these principles in all our affairs.

When reading these steps I replace the word alcohol with food. You could replace the word alcohol with gambling, anger, shopping, whatever your addiction. Working these steps requires much effort and consideration in everyday living. It is not easy, by any means. Sometimes it's a real pain in the ass. Then again, nothing that is worthwhile is ever easy, which is why I believe there are so many weight issues today. Everyone wants to be thin, but only if it's easy.

I weighed my food on a scale as I had done at my very first diet program. This way, I would know exactly what was going into my mouth meal by meal. Every morning I wrote down what I was going to eat for the day. Every day, three times a day, I weighed the food I had written down. This seemed a bit harsh and time consuming, all this weighing and writing down. However, looking into other food programs and calling nutritionists I found that mostly all food-related programs suggested keeping a daily journal and weighing portions, so I stuck to it. I hated the scale -HATED it! Four ounces of protein never seemed large enough. And what did it matter if I ate seven or fifteen ounces of carrots? I felt ripped off, like something had been stolen from me, but desperateness kept me honest. Not willpower, desperateness.

I experienced withdrawals from sugar and flour. The first two weeks in program I was extremely irritable, tired, weak, and shaky. I couldn't sleep and growled at my family. Though I was told withdrawals might happen, I found it hard to believe that giving up certain products would cause me to react this way. I didn't realize that my body and mind had become dependent on these products as a means of survival. I was used to ingesting whatever amount I wanted whenever I wanted it. Then I thought about coffee drinkers. How does a person who is used to two cups of coffee each morning react without coffee for just one day? How about the smoker? The one time my husband quit smoking I begged him to start again because I couldn't deal with his many moods. So it did make some sense, but it didn't make it any easier. I felt vacant, like a hollowed out chocolate Easter bunny.

Two months passed and I was sitting pretty in size 8 pants, feeling quite satisfied with myself. So, what do I do now? The holidays were coming and fancy desserts were just around the corner. Without sugar in my life to dull my senses I was suffering. I felt vulnerable and naked, like an open sore. Not a pretty picture, but the closest description to accurate I can think of. A festering wounded open sore. I was not physically bingeing, but was emotionally bingeing twenty-four hours a day. My life was a whirlwind. Small problems were big problems. Big problems were disasters. What the hell was the matter with me? Why wasn't I ever satisfied? I was thin, wasn't I? Isn't that all I ever wanted to be? Why then, was my life still one big mess, if not messier, now that I had lost the weight?

The Twelve Steps

It was not a requirement that you study or follow the steps to belong to the Program, but it was a strong suggestion that everyone give the steps a try. Without studying the steps, I was told the Program was just like any other diet program. It worked for as long as you worked it. The twelve steps promised to help with my big fat head, acting as a glue to keep me together.

My insecurities and fears were still running my life. Even though I was thin and had been now for a good year, a stressful situation would cause me to feel fat and insignificant. The steps promised to remove these feelings. The next sections are my own take on the twelve steps as I have grown to understand them.

Step One

Iwas a bit cynical, to say the least, when I first began what I consider the journey that introduced me to myself. Step one was to admit I was powerless over food and my life had become unmanageable. Now I knew that this was true, but had to disagree with the general consensus, or at least my big fat head did. I decided my life was not unmanageable. My lifestyle was just fine, thank you. So it had a few dings in it, nothing that couldn't be worked out. I know I said just a few paragraphs before that my life was a whirlwind, but that was a few paragraphs ago. I've grown since then. Maybe I could readjust, you know, get used to living in a whirlwind.

How could I admit out loud such a thing as being powerless over food? My psychology background told me if I admitted it was a problem then I would have to confront the problem. Plus it sounded silly and freakish to declare such a thing as food powerlessness. So my big fat head told me to keep quiet.

The thing I failed to mention was that in my heart I knew that this was not just about food powerlessness but also about life powerlessness.

I wasn't sure I was prepared to rip up a house, foundation and all, and begin from scratch.

When step one was finished the group was asked to make a commitment. The commitment was to agree that we were powerless over food, and life was unmanageable when binge eating. I agreed and said yes because I didn't have the nerve to go against the group, but inside my big fat head was telling me otherwise.

We moved on to step two: Came to believe that a Power greater than ourselves could restore us to sanity. This was a problem. *I* restored me to sanity. I'm the one who stopped eating sugar. I'm the one who suffered, who went through great pains to lose this weight. I restored myself. This *is* sacrilegious I just know it. I'm going to be zapped for being in this weird group.

I was told this was a step of faith that required a willingness to believe I could be restored because God could and would hear me, if I asked Him. When the commitment came round for step two, I said yes and waited for the lightening bolt.

Step three was more uninteresting babble. Step three: Made a decision to turn our will and our lives over to the care of God as we understood Him. Why should I? Aren't I responsible for my own behavior? Isn't this another weak man's statement? These people are copping out, that's what they're doing. They don't know shit. Then someone got up and said something like this: "I'm not asking you to suddenly believe in God, I'm just asking you to try to make an effort to turn over your will, to try not to be in control all the time, to accept life on life's terms. If you are having a bad day, give it to God, or your Higher Power as you understand Him." I don't believe I'd ever done that. When I was having a bad day I cursed God, I didn't turn to him for help. I thought He was the one doing it to me as a punishment because I deserved to be miserable. And I never thought of actually asking God for help on a daily basis. He was too busy to help me everyday.

The other aspect of step three that I considered important is that it didn't ask an agnostic to believe in God. It asked that no matter what you believed, to believe in a force greater than yourself. It made perfect sense to do that since I had been depending on myself all these years and look at the mess I had gotten into. Step three was a step of action. It says when life gets tough, give it to your Higher Power. That is not sedentary. It requires great effort to remove yourself from the control panel and step aside. You can't control someone dying, or the mail being late, or the cashier's attitude at the supermarket, but you can control how you react to these situations. You can turn it over to your Higher Power. And if your Higher Power is a popsicle stick, hey, fine by me.

Satisfied I wasn't going to rot in the depths of hell for working these twelve steps, I decided to study them honestly and with an open mind. Screw my big fat head; I was bucking my own system!

After rejecting my big fat head's thoughts, I realized that this was a spiritual program. One based on empowerment and faith. Step four: Made a searching and fearless moral inventory of ourselves. Notice the words *fearless* and *moral*. This was going to be no small task and would require a full month of self-examination and writing. Had I known what step four entailed before my decision to study the steps, I may have chosen a candy bar.

Step four was just what it said, writing down a personal inventory. The inventory was usually done in the form of an autobiography, and began chronologically. It was tedious, and brought up many issues I did not care to remember. It caused restless sleep and anxiety, and all-around confusion. I thought this was supposed to help me, but it seemed to be making me worse. I was told it was part of the process of getting through things. Oh, I understood now. *This* was walking through the pain. Moaning and groaning all the way to a piece of paper, I began to write my inventory. As I wrote I felt myself reliving each stage of my life, the hurt, the tears, the joy, and the food. The food. It was always there, for as long as I could remember. My safety net of satisfaction. Could it be true that I was powerless over it? Had I abused food so badly that it had become a block in my life? Had it stunted my growth in other areas by taking up so much of my time that there was no time to look at anything else? Had I really done that to myself?

I began to look forward to writing about my life. It wasn't anything remarkable, but it was worth looking at, I supposed. And no deep seeded memory surfaced. I did recall a few lost memories of sadness, emptiness and fear. But I also felt forgotten memories of happiness, memories of gratitude. It was like self-hypnosis on paper, real wild stuff.

Step five wanted me to admit to God, to myself, and to another human being the exact nature of my wrongs. That meant 'giving away' step four, reading or talking about what I had written down. O.k., telling God quietly in my own room is fine. But why do I have to drag a human into this? Why does someone else have to know my problems, my life story? Feeling like an obedient student, I chose a friend in the program and gave away my fourth step. Those who aren't familiar with the twelve-steps probably don't understand why a group of seemingly sane, reasonably intelligent people would gather in a room and look at our faults, our fears, and our dreams. Why we would torture ourselves with the past and fight for sanity in the present. Why someone who didn't seem so bad off would suddenly turn their emotional life upside down by the process of self-examination. *I* wasn't even sure why I was doing it. For self-improvement? I mean, let's face it, who has time for self-improvement with our busy schedules? Denial's a much easier avenue. Of course, I did follow through with this difficult task and it did feel good in the end. That's the thing about the twelve steps; you *always* feel good in the end.

Clearing The Path

Step six is a gentle, but difficult step: Were entirely ready to have God remove all these defects of character. All that is required of step six is a willingness to let go of your character defects and clear the path for a better way of life. That's the gentle part. The difficult part is letting go of your character defects and clearing the path for a better way of life. Saying you are prepared to make changes and actually making changes are two entirely different things.

To let go of my defects felt similar to hanging by a tight rope one hundred feet up while someone below yelled, "Jump with your eyes closed, I'll catch you!" Try to think of your defects as defenses created to combat life's stresses. These defects are intertwined with our personalities and are an integral part of our being. One of my defects was fantasizing. My reward for fantasizing was the illusion that I was important, always the hero of my story. This prevented me from addressing the real issues at hand, one issue being my weight.

Another habit of mine was having at least two different tasks continually going on at once. These tasks can either be large or small. As a rule, I grow bored easily and prefer to keep myself busy or face the wrath of my big fat head. When I became stressed, I added more and more tasks to my life covering up the real worry, even if it was a little worry. The next thing I knew, I suddenly had to drive two hours north to a specific store that had the exact product I needed to buy. Not wanted to buy, but *needed* to buy. I would impulse buy without thought and then regret it. This is where step six comes in. It asks that you think. It wants you to dissect your whole being and throw away the invisible corrosion of the past. It then asks that you fill up the empty holes with faith, positive thinking, and the rest of the eleven steps. Think of it this way: when an apple has a brown spot on it you peel it off, you don't throw the whole thing away. That's step six.

Step seven: Humbly asked Him to remove our shortcomings. To do this requires an acceptance of a power greater than ourselves and to ask this power to take away what it is about ourselves that fails us. My worrying, anxiety, and, as my husband puts it, my 'gloom and doom' attitude were all obstacles preventing me from living life to the fullest. I anger easily, and forgive sparingly. These shortcomings were not only unpleasant to my family, but they failed me. *I* failed myself with my attitude.

Step seven is a step of awakening. It allows you to see your behavior and reactions to situations objectively. Once you are aware of your patterns of behavior, you are free to change them, if you choose not to deny them. They give you permission to say, "I'm not perfect, help me to grow."

Step eight: Made a list of people we had harmed, and became willing to make amends to them all. This was a doozy. It wasn't writing them down that was hard, it was remembering *why* I was writing them down. Even if it was a little slight, a white lie, a sin of omission, I wrote it down. The main idea of step eight is to learn how to forgive others and ourselves. I was on my own list to apologize to. I had to learn how to forgive myself for all those years of mental anguish, character assassination, and denial of reality.

We were asked to look at our written list and from it choose one person with whom to make amends within a few weeks time. I decided to make an amends to my girlfriend about a situation that occurred eight years earlier. I thought this amends would be easy. I'd just say, "I'm sorry about my behavior eight years ago." And she'd forgive me, and that would be that.

Step nine: Made direct amends to those people, except when to do so would injure them or others. My girlfriend came to my house with a general idea of what I was going to say. I began choking on my words, unable to apologize. It took me forever to tell her I was sorry. The humility I had to conjure up was a blow to my ego. And this was the *eas-*

iest amends on my list! She'd long forgotten about my behavior, I was the one who was living with the guilt of my own conscience. She hugged and forgave me. I felt embarrassed that eight years ago I had acted in such a petty manner, and was glad that the person I was then was not the person I am now.

The studying of the twelve-steps was beginning to change me from the inside. Rebuilding your character is slow, steady work, but the results are worth it.

Step ten required that we continue to take personal inventory, and when we were wrong, promptly admitted it. This is a follow-up step to the previous nine steps. It asks that you think about your behavior and your responses to other's behavior towards you on a daily basis. To say, "I'm sorry" as soon as you realize an apology is necessary. Anger and resentment can't fester when you immediately apologize. I actually found myself saying, "This is what I would usually do, but what should I do now?" This daily evaluation of my behavior unlocked a part of me I didn't know existed: self-control.

Steps eleven and twelve worked together. Step eleven required meditation, prayer and improving a conscious contact with a Higher Power, praying for knowledge of His will for us and the power to carry out the will. Step twelve was to carry our message of recovery and tell others of our spiritual awakening while continuing to practice the twelve-steps in all our affairs.

I was familiar with meditation and quite adept at it. It had become almost a daily ritual for the past year. Other daily rituals included saying my prayers. At first I didn't want my husband or children to see me because I was embarrassed. Funny, I wasn't embarrassed to eat a half-gallon of ice cream in front of them, but I *was* embarrassed to kneel by my bed at night to pray!

Studying the twelve-steps with a group took fourteen months. I no longer thought them to be a hoax. I understood what all my hard work was for, what gift I received for my efforts. The gift of self-preservation. I had not binged on food in almost two years, a personal world record. The past fourteen months had given me hope that somewhere deep inside was the person I never knew I was. She wasn't fat, she wasn't mean or hard or spiteful. She was soft and kind and frightened. Still very, very frightened to show herself. But at least she was there. Amen.

My Sugar-Free Accomplishments

There were benefits that came when the bingeing ended. My obsessive-compulsive behavior dramatically decreased when I stopped bingeing. I hadn't realized how obsessive-compulsive I was until I remembered all the little rituals that I had to accomplish to make it through the day. Don't step here, step there, check and recheck the door to make sure it's locked, turn the bathroom light on and off four times. My obsessive thoughts and fantasizing had also decreased dramatically. I didn't need to fantasize about a better life when I was living one.

To show up at functions and holidays not worrying about how much I was going to eat was a blessing. These may seem trite accomplishments, but for me they were huge. My body image wasn't ruling my life and I not only appeared functional, I *was* functional. I chose the simple act of putting my food on a scale and I became 'normal'. Go figure.

So, Am I Cured?

Hate to say 'fat chance', but it was true. Did I still want sugar? Hell, yes. I could cry over how much I wanted sugar, which was no big surprise considering it was my main vice for twenty-eight years. The thought of a chocolate cake with chocolate frosting with maybe just a bit of chocolate shavings sprinkled on top—ahhh! Who wouldn't that cure?

I continued to go to Program meetings that discussed how people, one day at a time, refrained from eating those foods that cause them to overeat. The tremendous support and acceptance the program provided for me was emotionally overwhelming. Program is my extended family; the family who judges not, and understands fully.

Two and a half years had passed since I first entered Program. I attended two to three one and a half-hour meetings a week, weighed my food three times a day, and wrote down what I was planning to eat every morning. I also made phone calls to other Program members, at least three a day. I got up early to receive calls from sponsees and called my sponsor. This entailed a forty-five minute time slot in the morning. Getting my children off to school was becoming difficult with all the phone calls and preparation. It was getting to be too much work to take time out of my life to care for myself. My big fat head was beginning to work its magic.

I still felt left out during the holidays or at functions. I ate before a function since they were usually held in the middle of the afternoon. While everyone else was eating, I was sipping my diet coke or seltzer water. And then there were the innumerable questions: "Why can't you eat this, what harm would once in a while do?" "Why don't you just try it?" "Are you still doing that diet thing?" I could not seem to explain that I was not on a diet, but a food plan for life. If I asked them to pretend I was a diabetic, they would see how foolish the questions sounded. People really do only understand things in terms of medical emergencies when it comes to well being. We only take care of ourselves if and when a doctor says so, and even then we all 'cheat a little' with the food or the cigarettes or the alcohol. We can easily rationalize away our health for choices that only momentarily satisfy.

Many a diet program will tell you it's o.k. to eat a small amount of anything, as long as you don't abuse it. I beg to differ. If a woman from a diet center were to tell me I could eat sugar, she would actually be doing me more harm than good, because I would love to believe that I could have two cookies and walk away without giving it a second thought. This did happen to me in other diet programs and I became a victim to the diet desserts, bingeing helplessly on them. This is not to say that some people can't have two cookies, but it *is* to say that I can't, which was information I had to learn on my own. When I gave up sugar, I gave up the struggle to lose weight.

Sponsors

Sponsors are people in program who have been maintaining abstinence from compulsive overeating for at least three months. They are not doctors or nutritionists, but other compulsive overeaters sharing their experience. Anyone in Program can be a sponsor and the people we sponsor are referred to as 'sponsees'. A friend in Program gave my favorite description of what sponsoring entails. She said she considered herself "the keeper of information."

I consider having a sponsor imperative to the success of abstaining from compulsive overeating. A sponsor's job is to guide a person who is new to my Program with food plans and recommendations. A sponsor can give suggestions on where to go to meetings or what kind of literature would be beneficial to recovery. A sponsor can connect you with other Program members so that you don't feel isolated. A sponsor is someone who is willing to talk with you on the phone daily, if necessary. What you talk about is up to you. In short, a sponsor's sole purpose is to listen.

My Program comes equipped with tools of recovery. One of the tools is called a plan of eating. It suggests that people who are entering Program see a certified nutritionist to help them decide on a food plan. In the past sponsors were the ones who gave out food plans, but since the revision, more emphasis is placed on seeking professional help. I am a firm believer in letting the professionals take care of the nutritional aspect of the Program. The key to having a sponsor is to know that any-time during the day you can pick up the phone, dial a number and the person on the other line is just like you, a binger who is not bingeing, at least not today.

Levels Of Addiction

Just as there are high and low functioning alcoholics there are high and low functioning compulsive eaters. We've heard of the five hundred-pound person who can't get out of bed or the anorexic that can't hold up her head because she's too weak. We know at least one eternal dieter who switches from diet plan to diet plan searching for the plan that will work 'this time'. The eternal dieter may have a job, hold up the home front, and never appear frazzled. She can function in society, or at least she can fool them. Then we have the middle ground. Not quite bedridden, yet unable to get out of their pajamas, pull up the shades, or enjoy the day all because of a binge the night before. Perhaps calling in work due to the depression they are feeling from the binge. Functional-yet not. All these people are addicted to the same thing, but their levels of functioning are different.

Alcoholics may have specific drinks they prefer. Some like beer while others opt for hard liquor. The same applies to food addicts. Some like fried foods, others like starchy, some prefer sweet and others will eat anything as long as it is large in quantity. My friend who is an alcoholic didn't care what she drank to get high, as long as she got there. The same applies to food highs. For some people it's all in the journey, for others it doesn't matter how you get there, so long as you arrive.

What Do I Eat?

The eternal question of relatives and friends who want to lose weight is "What do you eat?" What I personally eat is not important. What is important to controlling my urge to overeat is weighing my food on a digital food scale and knowing what foods I can no longer tolerate, that is, foods that will eventually lead me into a binge. Weighing portions allows me to visually see that I am not overeating or under-eating. I know I've had enough because I weighed it. If a serving of oatmeal says 1/2 cup, then I measure 1/2 cup. No guesswork is necessary when a scale is used. This simple action frees me from allowing myself to say, "I don't think I ate enough at lunch, I think I'll have some crackers." I recall being told from my days at a diet center to watch every crumb that went into my mouth. And they were right, it wasn't mealtime that was the problem, it was all those little crumbs between that added up.

Reaffirmations That I'm Different

There will be people who refuse to take my addiction seriously. Could it be because if it were believed, a great amount of the population would see that it is in my shoes? Who wants to admit that food to some people is like drugs to others? It sounds silly. I can't tell you how many people have said that once they start eating chocolate, they can't stop, or a few potato chips just won't do unless they eat the whole bag. These same people are normal, healthy people who simply have certain foods trigger a reaction that causes the 'more' syndrome.

What causes me to believe that I am addicted to food, or more precisely, sugar? I treat sugar differently, have different emotions elicited at the site of a chocolate cake than a so-called 'normal' person would. Here's an example. I went to the movies to see "Titanic". My girlfriend's sister had bought chocolate mints and offered me some. I refused, but my girlfriend took two, *just two* small chocolate mints. When the movie started, I was still focused on the fact that my girlfriend took just two small chocolate mints and moved on with her life virtually unaffected. I was waiting for her to ask for more. Her sister nibbled at a few and put the box in her pocket. I almost couldn't stand it. Was she going to *save* the rest or something? How could they eat so little and be satisfied? Here I was watching what was supposed to be the best movie of the year and all I could think of was those damn chocolate mints. I wanted to scream, "Just eat the mint's, for God's sake, *eat them!*"

It is not normal to feel the same emotion toward a food product that one would feel toward a human being. I knew food was a problem because I coveted it. You don't covet food. It's just not right! I fought to the very end not to give up the bingeing. I waited until I was so miserable I couldn't stand it anymore. When it was time for me to quit a two-pack a day, six-year smoking habit I did it in one day. Never picked it up again. Not my drug of choice. Bingeing was my drug of choice. The image I try to present is not of a clinically obese person helplessly bingeing day after day. It's more of a woman anywhere from ten to thirty pounds overweight who needed to fill up her stomach so her head would shut off. And when her head needed to be shut off, her stomach was aching.

Even though the years go by and my desire is lessened, when the stress kicks in I still yearn for that new dessert I never tried. I still focus on the frosting my husband doesn't eat. I still dream about eating desserts when I'm going through a particularly hard life situation. It was a common reaction to binge under stress for so long that I now dream binge instead of reality binge. But I can't afford to go back to who I was, now that I know what my potentials are. I didn't see how else I could've fixed my eating behaviors. I couldn't fix what I couldn't control. So instead of trying to control it, I stopped eating it.

What I Don't Do To My Husband

My relationship with my husband has improved so much that it's hard to recall the abuse I used to put him through.

I don't beg him to go to the store or the ice cream shop with very specific instructions as to what I want. Because I don't do that, he doesn't have to come home having to explain they didn't have double chocolate, but he got me a vanilla. I don't scream at him for picking such a pathetic ordinary flavor as vanilla, and begrudgingly eat it anyway. I also don't have to call him a dope because after a while, if they didn't have my flavor, he decided not to bring me anything at all. He doesn't have to withstand more yelling because vanilla, although extremely boring in and of itself, is better than nothing.

I don't tell him he looks tired and should go to bed so I can sneak the food out from my hiding places and eat furiously at 10:00 p.m. I don't have to tiptoe to the freezer and hope the door doesn't creak when I open it. I don't have to hate my husband because he doesn't eat like me. I don't have to resent him because he can eat one or two cookies and be satisfied. I used to blame my husband because he wasn't like me. It was his fault he let me eat all those cookies, why didn't *he* stop me, why didn't *he* remind me, were my weekly statements to him. His reply, "because you'd have told me to shut up and mind my own business." And he was right.

Rewind

My big fat head told me that I was the only one who suffered and was misunderstood. It told me I was meant to be fat, would always be fat, and didn't deserve otherwise. I kept a scorecard the size of a football field of all the things that happened to me on a daily basis. I realized that to live in such a way was not conducive to my mental, spiritual, or physical health. So I took my knowledge of the twelve-steps, absorbed the support of my food program and fought back with all my might. I got thin, stayed thin, and continue to weigh my food. As for my big fat head, it's here somewhere peeking out every once in a while. It will always be with me, it's who I am. But I have learned not to give into its thinking as much. I said before there were no advantages to having a big fat head, but I was wrong. It took an awful lot of energy to listen to my big fat head. And now that I don't listen to it anymore I get to do other things with that energy.

BUT I WANNA BE A SUPERMODEL

It took thirty-two years, but I finally stopped believing anyone has the ability to look like a supermodel. That is, operation free. I was watching a television commercial about shampoo. The advertisement wanted you to guess which woman used the expensive shampoo and which woman used the cost effective shampoo. You weren't supposed to be able to tell the difference because both women had exceptionally beautiful hair. This meant that the cheaper shampoo was just as effective as the expensive brand. At that moment I thought, *"No, that's not right. Both woman have beautiful hair because they're lucky."* Let's face it; you have great legs because you were born with great legs. You can brush your teeth all day and still have dental problems, yet you have a friend who barely flosses and has never had a cavity. It's all in the gene pool. I expected to look like Cindy Crawford when I lost my weight. The magical transformation that never occurred was not only mind boggling, but also disappointing; until I realized that *my* imperfect body is just perfect for me.

Can It Be Prevented?

To wonder if something can be prevented before it starts is question-able. If I look to my childhood the tendency to overeat was there, but without the promise of anything definite. Many people start out as food-loving chubby children and end up thin adults. On the other side, many thin children grow up to be obese adults. It's a tough call. Alcoholics will often say one or both of their parents were alcoholics. My girlfriend's father is an alcoholic and her mother is a compulsive overeater. She has one sister and two brothers. She and her sister are compulsive overeaters, and one of her brothers is an alcoholic. Is this the result of learned behavior or genetics? I never could decide about the chicken or the egg.

Do I think my binges were a behavioral issue—yes. Do I think certain foods affect me chemically—absolutely. Do I think that for the rest of my life I will have this dormant food addiction to sugar that if activated will result in a compulsive binge? I believe so. According to some self-help books, once I take control of my life and accept myself in totality, the food cravings will disappear because I would have found out why I was eating. That's a beautiful concept and one whose bandwagon I'm quite willing to hop on. However, it seems far-reaching to believe that if I finally resolve this issue or that, my desire to eat compulsively will cease. So whether it is chemical, behavioral, or both, I seemed to have become so adept at bingeing that I don't think I'd be willing to try a cookie to test my capabilities.

Fast Forward

My main concern is for children and teenagers. Would they be willing to accept the fact that certain foods cause chemical cravings? One thing you do not want as a teenager is to be noticed for being different. Part of the fun of being a teenager is going to greasy food places with your friends on the weekends. Giving up what I loved was not easy as an adult. If given the choice as a teen, I'd have chosen the food. Mentally, I couldn't have possibly foreseen the ramifications for years to come.

A teenager in my family has a serious food problem; one a normal diet won't cure. I know this because of how he eats, how he covets his food, as did I. He once said to me that he would have to stop eating altogether to lose weight. He believed this was easier because the temptation would be erased completely. His remark chilled me to the bone as I pictured him going from overweight to anorexic back to overweight in later years. As a teenager and even as a young adult, I was infallible and had all the time in the world to worry about my future. I wouldn't have believed anything except *maybe* the possibility I could be addicted to sugar. And that bit of information would've done nothing to stop me from eating sugar. I would have shrugged it aside and continued with my life telling myself I would worry when I turned twenty or thirty or forty.

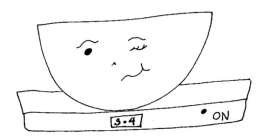

Weigh It

If I must stress anything at all, if there is one specific thing I can pass on to you it is this: WEIGH IT, WEIGH IT, and WEIGH IT! Weigh everything you eat on a digital scale and you will see remarkable results. Do not allow yourself to weigh cookies or ice cream if you are a sugar addict. Forget about potato chips if you are a starch freak. Don't weigh spaghetti if you can't eat eight ounces. Weigh your protein, weigh your vegetables, weigh your grains and weigh your fruit. By weighing what you eat you are weighing your own life. The two parallel each other. There will be no room for you and your big fat head to have mini-conferences throughout the day. A scale has the ability to tell your brain just how much you have eaten. This way your big fat head can't rationalize you are starving because you haven't eaten enough. You know you have eaten enough because you weighed your food. If you keep a diary of the weighed portions, that's even better. How can a big fat head argue with a black and white document?

These weighed portions you eat should come from a certified professional experienced in eating disorders. Your food plan should be personalized for you and your food should be kept simple. Remember, *do not, under any circumstances,* allow your big fat head to choose those foods you can handle. Let your mind do that. You may not be happy with the results, but they will be honest results. Only *you* know what you can't eat. The rest of the world can't cure you; we can only support you.

Play

My physical recovery came fast. My mental and spiritual recoveries are still in progress, and probably always will be. I have learned not to eat over people, situations, or personal emotions. I don't look forward to locking myself in the house with the shades pulled down on a sunny day to a feast of chocolate chip cookies and ice cream. I know with all my heart the seriousness of my eating disorder or disease or whatever it may be termed. No one alive could convince me that all would be well if I just ate in moderation. I would love (almost too much) to say I would be able to have just two cookies or a slice of cake a few years down the road. I'm not worried about the calories a cookies has, I'm worried about the mental anguish one cookie causes.

I'm not a professional in eating disorders. I claim no diet or food plan to be the number one cure-all. I do feel strongly that those foods that cause one to overeat (no matter what those foods are) should be eliminated from your diet if not permanently, then temporarily. It would certainly be difficult for a drug addict to give up heroin if he were still getting daily inoculations in his system.

I have controlled my bingeing by recognizing those foods I can no longer eat, mainly sugar foods. I have a support group and live life one day at a time. I keep a grateful list and get down on my knees twice a day and thank the Lord for the gifts I have been given. My physical recovery would not work without a mental and spiritual change. If I lost weight without changing mentally or spiritually I would be thin with the same big fat head. Eventually, I would turn back to bingeing to control the emotions that I didn't know how to handle. I ate all those years of my life away because I allowed myself to get into a pattern of thinking that was detrimental to my spirit. The way my mind buzzed around in my head all day in a thinking fury was pure insanity. My mind can still do this, only now I have the means to help myself through it not with food, but with the twelve-steps.

I am not perfect, and am glad for that. I still scream in my house, still have a short fuse and still experience anxiety and panic, only on a much smaller scale. I am not superwoman. I have all the vulnerabilities of a mother with three children worrying about bills, family safety, and the question of whether I am doing life 'right'. The difference today is I know this thinking is normal, whereas a few years ago I would've thought it wasn't. Then I would've eaten from frustration and insecurity.

In my most humble opinion, the most important step in recovering from compulsive overeating or bingeing or food addiction is not putting the food down: it's *wanting* to put the food down. And this want has to come from the pit of your soul, and you have to be ready to unleash all the demons that have been hidden there, in secret, for years and years. And to recognize that these demons are nothing but years of suppressed emotions will be the key that starts you on a personal path to freedom.

There's no big diet secret and no miracle pill. There's just a willingness from inside and an acknowledgement that you have *allowed* yourself the luxury of forfeiting your feelings to an addiction. You have the ability to change if you want to get better. All you have to do is let go of any expectations you had of yourself and your life, and start from there. Piece of cake!

A Word On Faith

I was sitting in church listening to a sermon when it suddenly struck me that faith is invisible. You can't see it and you can't describe it. You can't even feel it, at least not in a tangible way. Faith is something you sense, something you live and breathe. You can't buy it or give it away. One attains faith by his or her inner belief system. It has to be self-created with a firm foundation. You have to maintain a vision that you are but one remarkable piece of a very vast universe that a universal power (I call this power God) has created. This universal power is infinitely aware of each and every part of His universe and can restore even the biggest beasts, if they open their minds to Him. Can you believe this? Can you let yourself believe that from the beginning of your life there was a Higher Power watching over you, guiding and protecting you? That's faith. I feel faith is imperative to the process of any recovery. Faith in something is necessary, what that something is, is up to you. I chose God as my source of faith and discuss my faith as it correlates with God.

I read somewhere that fear and God do not live in the same house. Well, faith and God do. The wonderful part of having faith is the realization that you don't have to carry around your fears in a luggage bag. Give them to God (remember step three). If you possess such faith you must know that you, yourself, are not actually in control. Of course you control your own actions, thoughts and beliefs. But on a larger scale, you have no control. This is very good news for those of us with big fat heads. All along we thought we had to carry the burden when in reality someone much greater would have helped us if we had asked.

I thought I was a great follower of God, someone who possessed the greatest faith – blind faith. By blind faith I mean the kind of faith that no matter what happens; deaths, great financial losses, physical conditions such as becoming paralyzed for life, that you still maintain faith and know that you will be taken care of by your creator. Years ago an incident happened where a boy on vacation was shot in the head and killed. His father was, in my opinion, too forgiving and publicly forgave the wrong doers who were asking for his forgiveness. I watched in awe as this man talked about his gratitude for being fortunate enough to have known his son for as long as he did. I was *actually* angry with the father for being so forgiving. I understand now that the man was not dismissing any wrongs. What he realized is that he wasn't the Creator, it wasn't his business to judge or condemn. By forgiving the shooter he released himself and brought peace into his own life. That, in my opinion, is the greatest faith there is; blind faith.

Do I possess such faith? No I do not, although more and more I can feel God's presence working in my life. I'm still trying to keep up with the Jones' and fall victim time and time again to the blame game. Who can I blame for this? Who's going down for that? I have to reaffirm on a daily basis that God is with me and He will take care of me. I have to give my children's well being to God, my house to God, and my problems to God. I turn it all over to God on a daily basis, lest I forget and end up with my face in a bowl of hot fudge.

Although you can't be given faith, you can borrow someone else's. Look around, whom do you admire? Do as they do. Fake it until you make it. I took bits and pieces of people from my program that I truly admired for their strengths *and* failures and I borrowed their faith until my foundation was built. Build your foundation.

Eleven Pieces Of Advice

1.   Keep it simple. That includes the foods you eat, the day you plan, and the offers you decide to commit to. Don't complicate your life any more than is necessary by increasing your workload so that the only time you have left to yourself is bedtime. Love yourself enough to give yourself at least fifteen minutes of alone time, even if you have to lock yourself in the bathroom to do so.

2. Practice humbleness. Believe that you are not the center of the universe, but a part of it. The world's sole purpose is not to take care of you. That job is yours, and yours alone. Don't be afraid to get down on your knees and thank God or your Higher Power for the life you have been given.

3. Avoid harboring resentments. Does Suzie really know she hurt your feelings two years ago? Think of resentments as stuck balls of energy all over your body causing muscle aches, joint pains, and other problems. Practice releasing these balls during meditation times. Watch as they float upward toward the sky. Get rid of them.

4. Know what causes you to hang on to your addiction. Do this through writing, remember step four. Get in touch with your feelings every day, every second if necessary. When the need to eat arises get out a piece of paper and write, "I want to eat because…." Then write "If I binge I will feel…", Usually that's enough for me not to take that first bite.

5. Ask for help. Find a diet program or support center that works for you. Not everyone may have to find a twelve-step program or delve into the recesses of their soul to lose weight. Exercise, eat healthy, and honor your body. Everyone is different and should base their diet on their specific needs. No one should have to go through the difficult task of ending an addiction alone. It's impossible.

6. Rely on a power greater than you. To believe I am forgiven for my past sins and that I have a loving God who will take care of me is a great relief. Find a Higher Power and stick with it. There is something to be said for absolution.

7. Laugh. Laugh when your kid spills milk or when you trip over a toy that was supposed to be picked up. It's better than screaming and your mind will respond more positively with laughter rather than anger. Laugh at yourself when you feel like a fool.

Laugh at the silliness of an argument that happens when you and your spouse are tired on a Friday night. Laugh at life and minimize the worry. Laughter is one of the greatest tools to overcoming negative thinking. I have recently decided that when I am frustrated I will smile, and it works. I lie down at night with a bundle of worries and an exaggerated smile on my face. Eventually my worries are lifted.

8. Don't lie to yourself. You know who you are, so get over it. It is time to stop feeling sorry for yourself and start working towards controlling your life. Take a good long look in the mirror. What do you see? What's been hiding there? You know; you have *always* known. Stop saying, "I can't, I can't". I know it's not easy coming to terms with your big fat head. I have one myself. Have faith.

9. Worship something. Worship God, worship Buddha, worship Jesus. Create a shrine for your object. Place pretty objects around the shrine such as candles or incense or flowers. Write letters to your statue asking for help and place them near the shrine. Remove yourself from the control panel and give away the emotions that feed your big fat head. You don't need them anymore. Like I said before, if a popsicle stick works, go for it.

10. Learn to visualize what you want to get rid of. Brush away negative thoughts with visualization techniques. You can visualize a broom sweeping over you brushing away the black negative goop. Or you can visualize the negative goop floating up and out of your body like black snowflakes, only backwards. You can visually scrape it off, or wash it off or scoop it off. Replace the black goop with white snowflakes coming toward you or a white fluffy cloud or a white mist spraying gently over you. There's a lot to be said for visualization and meditation. Try it and remember, have faith.

11. Weigh it. I cannot stress enough the importance of weighing your food. By weighing your food you are weighing your life. Your life

was to binge or to not eat or to purge. Weighing food allows you the freedom to see the amount of food that you ingest on a daily basis. Keep a journal of your food as a basis to look at what foods you can and cannot tolerate.

What Next?

My life was not my own five years ago. I was ruled by binges and emotions and fears. I allowed myself to think the worst, to forget my dreams and to live in unhappiness. I suffered and my family suffered as a result of my big fat head. I thought this was my destiny. I was always going to be an unhappy overweight person who couldn't stop bingeing. I dismissed my mental, physical and spiritual health all for a bite of a brownie. The invisible pain this type of behavior caused is too powerful for words. My big fat head played the role of "Mommy Dearest" and I took the backseat. Now, for the most part, I am in the lead. I control my food and my thoughts. It is an uphill battle, I must admit. I lived a certain way for a very long time, I don't expect to transition easily after years and years of bingeing.

I have been given the gift of motherhood for the third time. This time I remained binge free and had a wonderful pregnancy and delivery, my easiest one. I don't pick at his food and we don't share snacks. I have my meals and he has his. He doesn't try to feed me because I've never tried to take any of his food. If he offers me something, which is seldom, I say "No thank you" or make believe I ate it to satisfy him. It is so wonderful to have the gift of abstinence. It pours over into every fiber of my being and every part of my life.

One of my biggest fears is self-exposure. I sit writing a book about what I consider pretty personal information and I'm afraid of self-exposure. I still don't want to pull that cloak off, the one that will allow you to see who I really am. But I feel I had no choice. I had to write this to heal myself and to help others. As I said in the beginning my honesty had to be first and was imperative to my survival, even if it hurt others. That also meant myself, knowing when the time came, when this book was finished, you would all know about me and my big fat head and that lardy goop that began oh so long ago. Truth be told, you probably knew anyhow. I was the one who was surprised; I never looked in the mirror. What about you? Go ahead—look in the mirror. And remember, have faith.

About the Author

Jodi Blase has a B.A. in Social Psychology from UMASS Boston. She has been free from binge eating for five years. She lives in Massachusetts with her husband and three children. This is her first book.